Do Your Parents Drive You Crazy?

Do Your Parents Drive You Crazy?

A Survival Guide for Adult Children

Janet Dight

PRENTICE HALL PRESS • *New York*

Published by Prentice Hall Press
A Division of Simon & Schuster, Inc.
Gulf + Western Building
One Gulf + Western Plaza
New York, NY 10023

PRENTICE HALL PRESS is a trademark of Simon & Schuster, Inc.

Library of Congress Cataloging-in-Publication Data
Dight, Janet.
  Do your parents drive you crazy?

  1. Adult children—United States—Psychology.
2. Parents—United States. I. Title.
HQ799.97.U5D54   1987   306.8'74   87-12577
ISBN 0-13-218686-1

Designed by Irving Perkins Associates

Manufactured in the United States of America

10 9 8 7 6 5 4 3 2 1

First Edition

To Mom and Dad, of course.

A Note to Parents of Adult Children

THE STORIES in this book all come from real people, but I've changed the names and other details so that no one, especially you parents out there, will recognize them. I know it might sound like your son who said the only time you want to see him is when your car needs repairs, or your daughter who said you stay so long when you visit that she feels like charging you rent, but it wasn't them.

Your children would never say anything like that about you.

Besides, I promised that you wouldn't be able to tell it was them. They said you'd be furious. Oops—I mean, I promised somebody else. Not your kids, somebody else. Honest.

—JANET DIGHT

Acknowledgments

I'D LIKE to thank the many people who helped me with this book:

- All the adult children who shared their stories with me— may this book provide them with some solutions and the knowledge that they're not alone.
- PJ Dempsey, who is not only my editor (again), but also my good friend.
- Jeanne Kramer, who went above and beyond the call of her duty as director of marketing for Prentice Hall Press.
- My agent, Merrilee Heifetz, who is "aggressive" in the very best sense of the word.
- Helen Kolb, who let me print her letter.
- Karen Robinson, who not only provided information and advice but also critiqued the manuscript.
- Rick, who is the reason I'm able to write anything.

Contents

Do Your Parents Drive You Crazy?

Introduction

FOR YEARS I went out of my way to make my parents happy. That wasn't too difficult since I lived only an hour's drive away. I visited regularly, I was successful in business, and I managed to avoid any of the major sins such as unwed pregnancy, arrest, or extended unemployment.

Then I moved to Colorado, some 1,352.7 miles away from my parents' home in Mansfield, Ohio, and relations got strained.

My mother (who handles all the parent-child communications in our family) couldn't understand why I didn't visit them every three or four months. She couldn't understand why I didn't come home every year for Christmas. She chose to ignore the fact that I had other obligations: a job, a fiancé, almost-in-laws who live in Colorado, and a stepson who spends every other Christmas with us— among other things. She never let a phone conversation or letter go by without asking when I was coming to visit.

When I did see my parents, they devoted the first half of my visit to discussing how long it had been since I had been there, and the second half to finding out when I was coming back. It was a one-two combination punch.

Then, during one trip to Ohio, for no reason I can put my finger on, I did a strange and unprecedented thing. Instead of making vague promises or changing the subject, as I usually did when the question of when I was coming back arose, I told my mother the truth. I said, "Mom, I can't afford to come back to Ohio two or three times a year. I don't have the money and I don't have the time. Each

1

trip costs over five hundred dollars and takes at least a week. You're asking too much."

I steeled myself for a hysterical reaction: What an ungrateful, thoughtless child I was; how they had done everything for me and the least I could do was visit them regularly; what was wrong with me that I didn't realize how much they missed me; and why did I have to live in Colorado anyway?

Instead, my mother said quite calmly, "I know. It would just be nice to see you more often." And to my surprise, that was the end of the conversation.

A few months later, while my father—who, I am convinced, will one day be installed in the Smithsonian Institution as an outstanding example of the Great American Complainer—was delivering one of his tirades, I said, as good-naturedly as possible, "Don't you get tired of being mad about everything?"

Again I expected a fight. But he just chuckled and said, "I do get riled up, don't I?"

What? No temper tantrums? No "Watch your mouth, young lady"? No sighing in disgust? What was going on here? I stood up to my parents, and the world didn't come to an end. It was a miracle.

It occurred to me that maybe I was on to something. Maybe there was a solution to the problem of being an adult child. Maybe it involved being more of an adult and less of a child with them. Maybe it involved seeing them as people instead of as parents.

And since everybody I knew had the same problem, but didn't have the faintest idea what to do about it, maybe there was a book in it.

And sure enough there was.

Now, I'm not a psychologist, so this is not a psychological book. It's just a book of practical advice that's designed to let you know that almost all of us adult children have problems with our not-so-adult parents, and that even though it may not seem possible, there is hope.

This book is based not only on my experiences but on those of hundreds of people I've talked to. Even so, I think my parents are a little nervous about what I'm going to say about them.

My mother has told me three hundred times in the last year what a wonderful mother she was, that she has no regrets about how she raised me, that she did the best she could, and that she knows I won't say anything bad about her. It's funny, but prior to my getting this book contract, she had never mentioned any of that.

Here's a sample of our recent correspondence on this subject:

May 12
Dear Janet,
    You know we don't care what you write about, as long as what you write <u>sells</u>. [*Sells* was underlined three times.] By the way, here's a letter from my friend Helen.

Love,
MOM

Dear Gladys,
    I'm so glad to hear about Janet's new book. I only hope she doesn't do to you and Ken what that awful Patti Davis did to her parents. The terrible things she said about Ron and Nancy! Anyway, Janet has no business saying anything bad about you and Ken. You two were perfect parents.

All my best,
HELEN

Naturally, I took this as a hint, so I wrote back to my mother:

May 20
Dear Mom,
    Thanks for Helen's letter, but you don't have to worry. As I've told you before, this book isn't about you and Dad. It's a

general how-to book for adult children. I won't pull a Patti Davis or a *Mommie Dearest* or anything else on you.

Besides (ha, ha), wire hangers never seemed to bother you.

Love,
JANET

June 15
Dear Janet,

I can't believe you thought I sent you Helen's letter to "drop a hint." I *thought* you'd think it was funny. Obviously, you've lost your sense of humor.

And I don't use wire hangers.

Signed,
YOUR MOTHER (WHO RAISED YOU PERFECTLY)

Senses of humor are sometimes scarce in my family.

My father hasn't said too much about this book. But I got my writing ability from him, and I'm sure he thinks I'm using it against him.

So to save my own hide, I'm not going to say another word about my own parents in this book. God knows I'll have enough trouble over what I've said about them in this introduction.

But if you look hard enough, you'll find them in here. They're just cleverly disguised.

Finally, in the interests of being thorough, I should mention that I've tried to be fair about apportioning blame between mothers and fathers. Some traits, however, are more typical of mothers, while others are more characteristic of fathers. But neither sex has a lock on these idiosyncrasies. For every "Mom" story, there's a Dad out there who does the same thing—and vice versa.

And although I refer to parents throughout this book, I know that some of you, because of death or divorce, may have only one. So please bear with me on the "Mom and Dad" stuff.

Now let's see what we can do with these old rascals.

1

The Tie that Binds

YOU'VE HAD IT. You've absolutely had it. If you get one more phone call from your parents that contains the phrase "it's been almost a month"—or "week" or "year" or "half hour"—"since we last saw you," you're going to scream. And if you hear them say one more time, "We know how busy you are, so don't worry about us (sigh), we'll get by somehow," you'll need major psychotherapy.

They've pushed you too far. You can't stand the guilt any longer, so you're going to do it. You don't want to, but you have to. You're going to visit your parents.

How gruesome.

You can picture it all now: the hours upon hours of mindless conversation, the stories you've heard a million times before, and the constant probing questions about whether or not you're *really* happy.

You'll be subjected to your father's continuing harangue about the morons in Washington who, if they think inflation is under control, ought to take a look at his utility bill, which (according to him) goes up 30 percent every month.

You'll have to endure trips to the grocery store with your mother, where she will wink conspiratorially at the checker and announce, "I've got to stock up; my baby is home for a visit." Then she'll give him a fifteen-minute rundown of your life history, your educational background, and your professional credentials. Next time, she promises, she'll bring pictures of your children.

A shudder of apprehension runs through you. It's too much for any one human being to have to bear. I mean, you love your parents and all, but after a couple of hours with them, you're begging for mercy: "Please don't tell me how thin I used to be. Please don't make me explain again how to work the VCR I bought you for Christmas in a moment of sheer madness. Please don't make me spend hours and days pretending I'm having a good time here."

Try to get hold of yourself.

Seeing your parents won't be that bad. All right, so the last visit wasn't any great shakes, and for weeks afterward the mere sound of your parents' voices on the phone set your teeth on edge, but it doesn't have to be like that. These visits don't have to be agonizing. You're a reasonably intelligent adult; if you try hard enough, you can make this one go well. After all, it *has* been a long time since you've seen your parents. You should be looking forward to a visit with them.

You promise yourself that this visit will be different. No more squabbling, no more teeth-gritting, no more being offended when your parents grill you about how much money you make or when you're going to have more (or any!) children. No, this visit will be enjoyable and fun. This visit will be everything Miss Manners, Dear Abby, and Norman Rockwell say it should be.

Even if it kills you.

So you call your parents and tell them you're coming, and their joy is boundless. Your mother is near tears at the thought of seeing her little darling again.

What a wonderful child you are to make your parents so happy.

You hum a little tune while you're packing your suitcase. You imagine good food, lots of attention, and a chance to sleep in your old room again. It will be wonderful.

But as you drive into your hometown and head up your parents' street, doubts begin to creep in. Is a pleasant, normal, sane visit with your parents really possible? Have you been kidding yourself, maybe just a little? Think, now, haven't you made the "happy visit" resolution before? Hmmm. You vaguely remember planning other pleasant visits in the past, other visits when it was going to be different and it was going to be great. But when you got there, it was never different, and it was never great.

Uh-oh, could this have been a mistake?

You pull into the driveway, and the instant your tires crunch on the gravel, the front door of the house flies open, and your worst fears are confirmed. Your mother races down the sidewalk, an overjoyed smile on her face, her arms waving wildly in the air—ecstatic at the prospect of clutching you to her bosom once more. Your father, in an attempt to counteract this euphoria, strolls leisurely down the sidewalk behind her, relighting his pipe as he goes and pretending not to notice the big impact you're having.

The sight of a sixty-year-old woman jumping up and down, squealing with delight, is frightening. You know you are about to be squeezed, pawed, slobbered over, evaluated, interrogated, nagged, talked to death, and—if at all possible in this one short visit—remade into a better human being.

You slump down in the car seat. You can't face this. You smile weakly out the window and wave at your parents to indicate you'll be out of the car in just one little minute. In slow motion, you put the car in "park" and pull on the emergency brake. You carefully straighten out the wheel so the tires are pointing exactly straight ahead, and make sure you've turned the key all the way to the "lock" position.

You slowly remove it from the ignition and methodically fold it back into the key case. Then, as if it were a cup of hemlock, you reach for the door handle.

"Oh, baby, you're home," your mother shrieks, two octaves above a normal speaking voice. "Oh, I can't believe you're finally home." She grabs you and plants a wet, sloppy kiss on your cheek. Your father stands back, puffing on his pipe and trying not to look too interested in your arrival. Your mother grabs your arm with both hands and says, "Did you have a nice trip?" She leans into your face and cries, "You look so good! Doesn't our baby look good, Daddy?"

Daddy mutters something unintelligible and continues puffing on his pipe.

"I'll, uh, just get my suitcase," you say, leaning toward the back of the car and trying to loosen the hammerlock your mother has on your arm.

"Don't worry about that," she says. "Your father will get it later." She drags you toward the house. "Mrs. Davis called and said to be sure to tell you hello when you got here. I've been telling her all about your promotion, and she's *so* impressed. Of course, why wouldn't she be? Her kids barely have jobs, let alone promotions. Her son has been—"

"Wait a minute, Mom," you break in. "Who's Mrs. Davis?"

"Oh, you know Mrs. Davis. She's in my bridge club, and her husband, Bill, goes fishing with your father—well, he does when he doesn't have a hangover. You wouldn't believe how that man drinks. I guess he doesn't do it on the job, but after work...."

"Mom," you repeat more firmly, "I don't know who Mrs. Davis is."

"Of course you do, dear," she says in her best "stop arguing with me" voice. "They live about three blocks from here. *I told you*, she plays in my bridge club." Once in the house, she breaks the death grip on your arm and rushes off to the kitchen, leaving you alone in the living room with your father.

"So, Dad," you begin vaguely, "how are things around here?"

"Fine, just fine." There's a long pause, then he says, "How's the weather out your way?"

"Wet. Real wet for this time of year." Long pause. "How's the weather been here?"

"Dry. Real dry." Long pause. "Hard on the lawn." He sits down in his favorite chair, puts the newspaper up in front of his face, and begins reading.

After that stimulating conversation, you work up a how-great-it-is-to-be-home smile and follow your mother into the kitchen, where a major-league buffet is in the making. "We didn't know exactly what time you'd be here," she says, even though you told her on the phone that you'd arrive no later than five o'clock, and would call if you got delayed. "So I thought we'd just have a little bit of this and that. You know, some hors d'oeuvres." You know your mother's hors d'oeuvres: chicken, shrimp, roast beef, potatoes, bread, and every dessert known to mankind. "Just wait till you taste this triple chocolate devil's food cake," she says. "Jean Franklin gave me the recipe, and it's absolutely delicious."

You don't know who Jean Franklin is, but you're not about to say so.

"Gee, Mom, I've, uh, really been trying to cut down on the sweets," you say carefully, trying not to hurt her feelings. "You know, sitting in the office all day, I don't get as much exercise as I used to."

She looks at you as if you've lost your mind. "Don't be silly," she says curtly. "I spent all morning making this cake. I'm sure one little piece isn't going to hurt you."

There goes your diet.

She surveys the buffet, and satisfied with what she sees, she says, "Are you ready to eat?"

"But, Mom, I just walked in the door."

"I think we'll eat in the family room," she says.

Oh, great, you get to eat off your lap and watch "Wheel of Fortune" at the same time.

Your mother heads for the family room to make sure the television is on. It is. At full volume. And at full psychedelic color. Everybody has green skin and orange hair.

Over dinner, and over the hysterical screams of the "Wheel of Fortune" contestants, your mother says, "So, tell us about your job." You start in, but nobody's listening. Now and then your father drags his eyes away from the television just long enough to mutter through a mouth full of food, a disinterested "That's good" or "Is that right?" Your mother doesn't stay seated for more than thirty consecutive seconds. "Wait a minute, dear," she says and runs to the kitchen to refill your dad's plate. "Wait a minute, dear," and she gets up to let the cat out. "Wait a minute, dear," and she gets up to put another pot of coffee on.

When she runs out of errands, she stares at your plate, not satisfied with how much you're eating. "Do you want more roast beef?" she asks, frowning.

"No, thanks, Mom, I'm stuffed."

"Are you sure?"

"Really, Mom, I'm fine."

"I just bought it this morning at Kerchman's, and they have the best meat in the world. " When you don't beg for more, she adds, "It's delicious," in that singsong tone of voice that means "Be a nice baby and eat for Mommy."

"No, Mom, I couldn't possibly eat any more."

"There's plenty here. Come on, have just one more tiny little piece. I cooked it just the way you like it."

Is she going to break into the "Open Wide for Maypo" song?

"Mother, I don't really want any more roast beef," you say through clenched teeth. "*Really.*"

Better change the subject. Maybe you can squeeze in a humorous office politics story before the prime-time TV

schedule begins. You tell—quite amusingly, you think—
how two of the managers in your department actually got
out rulers and measured their desks to see who had the
larger, and therefore the more prestigious, office furniture. "Do you believe these guys?" you ask with a laugh.

Your father sniffs in disgust. "That's the most ridiculous
thing I've ever heard," he says. "If these stuffed shirts had
to work for a living like I did for thirty years, they wouldn't
be so damn concerned about the size of their desks. I was
grateful I had a job, let alone a desk." He scowls. "Where's
the sugar?" He gets up and stomps into the kitchen.

"Don't mind your father," your mother whispers after
he's gone. She smiles. "He's so happy you're here."

How that follows is beyond you. What you're doing here
is also beyond you. In fact, how you can possibly be related
to these people is beyond you.

Okay, Dad's gone, but Mom's still here. Time hasn't completely run out for the pleasant-visit scenario. You can discuss your kids with her. That's one of her favorite topics.
You tell her how your two-year-old son, Johnny, keeps
beating up your cat. "We don't know what to do about it,"
you say. "He's really defiant about it. He doesn't think he's
doing anything wrong. Do you have any suggestions on
how we ought to handle it, Mom?"

"Johnny, defiant?" your mother says, incredulous. "I
don't believe it. He's an angel when he's here. Well, if I
were you, I wouldn't worry; he'll grow out of it. Why, just
look at you. You were a handful at that age, but look how
well you turned out."

That's true; you haven't beaten up a cat in years.

She listens for sounds from the kitchen, then sighs,
"Your father can't find the sugar." She jumps up to go help
Dad with this monumental task.

But she pauses at the door to the family room: "Can I
bring you some more roast beef? There's plenty left."

Ain't It a Shame

Now, isn't that pathetic? You look forward to seeing your parents, but the longer you're with them, the crazier they make you. Your mother panics when the weather's bad, for fear you'll be in a forty-seven-car pile-up on the way home. Your father keeps saying, "Considering how much we spent for your college education, it's too bad you have to work at that crummy health food store." They compare notes, as if you weren't in the room, on how your furniture could be better arranged, how you're not disciplining your children correctly, or what could be taking up so much of your time that you can't call them more than once a month.

Fifteen minutes after you walk through their door (or, worse, they walk through yours), you're ready to leave. You develop lockjaw, or you start talking in a sarcastic tone of voice you haven't used since high school. Your parents nag, and you give in as if you were seven years old, or they ignore you and you start turning cartwheels to get their attention. They get on your nerves, and you're afraid to say anything, or you start sniping at them, and sometimes the sniping blows up into a big argument in which everybody accuses everybody else of not caring.

And when the agony of the encounter is over, you hate yourself. You feel guilty. You know you shouldn't be so hard on them. They mean well. They can't help the way they are. They're old; they're going to die soon. If you were a really good son or daughter, you would try to make the best of what little time they have left. You wouldn't give them a hard time. You wouldn't wish you were somewhere —anywhere—else on the planet besides their house. You wouldn't let them get to you; you'd let their negative comments roll off your back. You'd understand that they're just concerned about you.

But you can't. They irritate you too much. So, mostly, you just avoid them.

Why Bother?

Should you try to straighten this relationship out? Is it worth it? Isn't it easier to let your life be disrupted now and then, be irritated, feel guilty about it, and then try to forget any of it ever happened?

Or maybe you should say, "Mom, Dad, I love you, but you drive me crazy, so from now on I'm going to visit you two afternoons a year, once in July and once in December. No calls, no letters, just noon to 5:00 P.M. on July fourth and December twenty-fifth. That's it. That's all I can handle."

Let's be honest: You love your parents, and what you want is a better relationship. Not seeing them, or continuing with this teeth-gritting approach, doesn't work. You want the comfort of being around people who genuinely care about you. You want to know that if the bottom really falls out, you have someplace to go and somebody to turn to. Your friends may give up on you, the government may or may not provide, but your parents will always be there.

Besides, your parents are your personal historians. They are your link to the past, your connection to your ancestors and your heritage. To the people you work with, you didn't exist before your (or their) first day in the office. To your neighbors, you didn't exist before you bought your house or moved into your apartment. To your friends, you didn't exist before they met you in college or at the neighborhood bar. But your parents remember you from the day you were born.

Yes, but They Drive Me Crazy

Okay, okay, so it's hard to maintain such a global perspective when your father tells you you're crazy for spending so much money on a pair of shoes, or your mother calls you into the kitchen for the 475th time to see what cute little thing the dog is doing. But every contact with your parents doesn't have to be a source of irritation. And every *failure* to contact your parents doesn't have to be the cause of guilt and self-recrimination.

Believe it or not, it is possible to get along with people who think you're still thirteen. You *can* have a better relationship with your parents, no matter how smothering, childish, neurotic, obnoxious, wishy-washy, or domineering they are now.

The formula for this transformation is quite simple: You start acting like an adult around your parents, and you train them (really!) to treat you like an adult. Putting this formula into practice is a bit more difficult, but that's what the rest of this book will tell you how to do.

You may not get all the way to warm, close, and loving with your parents, but you can definitely get to the point where you can see them without having a migraine headache. You might even get to the point where you enjoy them.

Irritation is nature's way of telling you something is wrong. If something's wrong with your relationship with these two very significant people in your life, don't you think you owe it to yourself and to your parents to fix it?

2

Who Are These People?

ENOUGH, ALREADY, of this "my mother," "my father," and "my parents" stuff. It's time to start treating your parents like *people*.

Yes, parents are people, too, but you probably don't have the faintest idea what kind of people they are. All you know is what kind of *parents* they are.

That's not altogether your fault. Chances are your parents haven't wanted you to see their real selves. They have an image to maintain, standards to uphold, an example to set. So for years they've put on an artfully designed "parent" act for you. They made sure you saw only what they wanted you to see. If they drank too much, had affairs, or goofed off at work, they were very careful to cover it up. They didn't tell you dirty jokes or admit that, when you weren't around, they didn't eat their vegetables. They wanted you to think of them as the perfect mommy and daddy.

Maybe You've Misjudged Them

All this covering up can trick you into thinking your parents are smarter, kinder, stronger, or more successful than they really are. But sometimes the facts don't support the illusion.

And if you're going to relate to them on an adult-to-adult basis, you'd better find out who the "adult" is on your parents' side of the equation.

"My mother had a rule that no one was allowed to bother my father with problems," said Jeff, a twenty-seven-year-old college instructor. "Dad was too busy, his job was too stressful, and he was supposedly above and beyond such mundane domestic matters. I broke my wrist one afternoon, and my mother actually refused to wake my dad up from his usual Saturday-afternoon nap. She hushed me up, drove me down to the emergency room, and Dad didn't find out until he got up and the 'emergency' was all over.

"Looking back, I realize it wasn't that Dad was too busy; it was that Dad couldn't handle problems. He got so upset whenever anything went wrong that he made the situation even worse. My mother took the easy way out: She didn't tell him about our problems until they had been solved."

On the other hand, this playacting can sometimes hide your parents' strengths and cause you to underestimate them.

Victoria, a highly successful businesswoman, had always thought of her mother as weak and ineffective. "She deferred to my father on everything—or so it seemed—and made a point of staying in the background. It annoyed me that she wouldn't do more with herself.

"When I was twelve, my mother took a job as a secretary for the city parks department. My dad didn't care, but my mother's friends were up in arms. They couldn't understand how she could leave her beautiful home and do something as despicable as work. But she didn't care. She couldn't understand how they could stay home all day and do nothing but supervise their cleaning ladies.

"It didn't dawn on me for years that, for 1964, this was pretty radical behavior—particularly in our ritzy neighborhood. It took a lot of courage on my mother's part to do what *she* wanted to do, instead of what was expected of her by her social circle."

Is This a Reliable Witness?

What your parents say about each other also contributes to the distorted image you have of them. They want you to feel, good or bad, the same way they do about each other.

Good marriages tend to breed positive—sometimes overly positive—comments, such as "Your father always put his family above his career" or "Making a nice home for us was the most important thing in your mother's life."

Bad marriages tend to do just the opposite: "Your father couldn't get promoted if his life depended on it" or "Your mother hasn't got a brain in her head."

But it's never that black and white.

Try to get past their opinions of each other as parents, and find out what they really think of each other as people. Why have they stayed married this long (I guarantee you it wasn't out of habit), or why did they get a divorce, if they didn't stick it out? If you can get to the *real* reasons they're involved or disinvolved with each other, you'll have a better understanding of who these people are.

Parents Unchained

Location is another factor. When you show up at your parents' house, especially if it's the house you were raised in, it's the old family back together again, and they automatically shift into their parent role. They feel responsible for meals, clean sheets, and how much sleep you get. They feel responsible for taking care of you.

To get a fix on the real "them," you'll have to get them out of the house, and take them to places that don't trigger the parenting urge. Take them out to dinner, to the mall, or to a movie—and watch how they act.

> "I took my parents to see the movie *10* a few years back," said Dave, a thirty-six-year-old architect, "even though I was afraid it would be too racy for my mother.
>
> "In one scene, Bo Derek tells Dudley Moore that she likes to have sex while listening to Ravel's *Bolero*—only Bo puts it much more bluntly. I cringed, but my mother burst out laughing. For hours after the movie she kept repeating the dialogue from that scene and cracking up. I couldn't believe it—my mother actually saying the 'F-word.' She was like a completely different person."

Once you get your parents out of the house, spend some time with them—not when you're being dragged around as this week's prize catch to be oohed and aahed over, but when your parents are just hanging out with their buddies. (Yes, parents have buddies, too.) Be a substitute on their bowling team. Visit your father's office, and take him and his colleagues out for a business lunch. Volunteer for a few hours at the hospital where your mother works.

Fit in as unobtrusively as possible, and watch how your parents get along with their friends. If you get a chance, take their friends aside, and ask what they think of your parents. You'll see a whole different side of two people you thought you'd known for years.

And keep asking yourself: What are their strengths? What are their weaknesses? How does what I see compare with the image of them that I've been carrying around all these years?

Can You Get Them to Change?

Seeing your parents as they really are, though, isn't enough. You have to *accept* them as they really are. That doesn't mean you have to like them, or approve of everything they do. It means you have to stop hoping they'll become something different.

One son laughed and said, "I don't worry about my mother changing. Her favorite activity is worrying about me. She'd never give that up."

"My father is an arrogant SOB," one daughter said. "You couldn't turn him into a decent human being with ten years of psychoanalysis and five million dollars."

"They'll never change," another claims.

For you to have a better relationship with them, they don't have to change. And that's fortunate, because they can't. They've been around for over half a century, and by now their personalities are carved in concrete. A grouchy old man who hates kids is not going to turn into a replica of Heidi's grandfather, no matter what you do. And you'll never transform a postmenopausal woman who's afraid to use an automatic teller machine into a Helen Gurley Brown. It ain't gonna happen.

But you can get them to treat you like an adult instead of like their long-lost child. Your parents have the capacity to act perfectly normal and civilized. They do it all the time around their friends, co-workers, and even total strangers. Your father doesn't tell his best golf buddy that *his* children are brats. Your mother doesn't say to her best friend, "For heaven's sake, do something with your hair." They *know* how to act reasonably. And if they can act that way toward other people, they can act that way toward you.

Don't Take It Personally

The bad news is that how your parents act around their friends is the best behavior you can hope for. It they're loud and obnoxious at the office, that's what you're stuck with at home. If they're quiet and shy, you can stop hoping that they'll be the life of your next party.

But whatever they're really like, let them be themselves.

They are separate people with separate lives. You shouldn't try to improve or correct them any more than you'd try to improve your boss's personality or correct your neighbor's behavior.

And stop worrying about how they make you look. Despite what you believed in junior high school (and may still believe), what your parents do is not a reflection on you. It's only a reflection on them. If your father wants to wear striped shirts, checked shorts, black socks, and sandals, it's —believe it or not—none of your business. (Besides, if your mother can't stop him from dressing like that, you certainly can't.) People may think he dresses weirdly, but nobody looks at his clothes and says, "Gee, this guy's kid must be a drip, too."

You're too old to be embarrassed when your mother goes to the grocery store with her hair in rollers, or when your father leaves a minuscule tip in a restaurant.

Just because you'd do it differently doesn't give you the right to insist that your parents do it your way—any more than they have the right to insist that you live life *their* way. At this late date, they are entitled to do whatever they want to with their lives. If you don't like it, you don't have to participate. But you have no right to badger them to behave "up" to your standards.

Let Your Parents Go On Without You

If you're lucky enough to have parents who decided to turn back into real people once you left the nest, don't resent it.

One woman complained that her mother was never home anymore. "Every time I call, there's no answer. It's annoying." I suppose it is, if you expect Mama to be breathlessly waiting by the phone in case you decide to give her a jingle.

And one son griped, "My mother got a job, and that was

the end of family holidays. On my last birthday, she invited us over, then called Domino's and ordered a couple of pizzas." How depressing to no longer be the center of attention, how sad that your parents' world doesn't come to a grinding halt anymore when their child—you—needs or wants something.

Come on, gang, it's time to grow up. You're not losing a couple of parents; you're gaining two potential new friends.

It's Never That Simple

Of course, just because you find out who your parents really are, don't expect them to yell "uncle" and give up the parent roles they cherish. You'll still have to deal with the mother who gives your house a white-glove inspection whenever she visits, or the father who doesn't remember what your major was in college but knows—to the penny —how much your education cost him. You'll have to cope with the mother who becomes hysterical when you consider moving to another city, or the father who thinks you're stupid because you didn't buy the same brand of lawn mower he bought.

Because there's such a vast assortment of exasperating parental types, it's necessary to put them in some sort of manageable order. Naturally, some parents, being multi-talented and having devoted a lifetime to the study of driving you crazy, cross the boundaries of these classifications with ease, and indeed belong in several or even all of the classifications simultaneously. But for our humble purposes, we'll use the following five categories:

1. The Perpetual Parent
2. The Users
3. The Manipulators

4. The Moaners-and-Groaners, the Mean-and-Nasties, and the Bullies

5. The Inattentive, the Distracted, and the Oblivious

A word of warning: Your parents will never take the initiative in improving your relationship with them. They were instrumental in setting up this relationship in the first place, and they've been active in keeping it this way. They like it. They like being the Parents, in charge of the Children, and being in a position of authority and control.

If you want change, you'll have to get it yourself.

3

The Perpetual Parent

THE PERPETUAL PARENT lives by the motto "Once a parent, always a parent." They treat you as if you still lived upstairs in the second bedroom on the right—you know, the one with the ragged posters on the wall and the six-inch-diameter dustballs under the bed. They think you need to be told what to do, what time to go to bed, what safety precautions to take in the big, bad world, and, most important, what time to call them on Friday.

Even if you're the forty-five-year-old chief of staff at the Mayo Clinic, or yourself a parent of six kids, your mother still thinks of you as her baby, and your father still thinks of you as that crazy kid who smashed in the fender on his brand-new 1972 Oldsmobile. Because you'll always be their baby.

Don't believe me?

Ask your parents how old you are. Seriously, call and ask them. Your conversation will go like this:

"Hi, Mom. Hi, Dad. How old am I?"

"What?" they'll ask, surprised and suspicious. What are you trying to pull here, anyway? "Don't be silly."

Don't let them off the hook. "I'm not being silly. How old am I?"

Don't give them any hints, like, "I was born the same year Dwight D. Eisenhower was elected president—no, the *first* time he was elected."

They'll dodge the question. "I don't know what's gotten into you," they'll laugh nervously. "If you don't know how old you are (ha, ha), we're certainly not going to tell you."

"I know how old I am," you say. "I want to know if *you* know how old I am."

It will take them a while to figure it out. "You were born in, let's see, uh, 1952? Yes, 1952, and this is 1987, so that would be...let's see, seven take away two is...no, that can't be right. Good heavens, you can't be *that* old."

"How old?" Make them say it.

"Well, thirty-five. You can't be thirty-five."

Confirm that you are.

"You are? Are you sure? I can hardly believe it. Isn't it amazing how fast time goes by? Why, it seems like just yesterday that you were going off to school."

They mean grade school, not graduate school.

"And I remember that cute little outfit you wore, and you had all your little pencils sharpened and lined up perfectly in your Mighty Mouse pencil box—you were such a little organizer—and..."

Brace yourself for a lengthy run down memory lane.

Somewhere in your childhood, at least as far as your parents are concerned, you stopped getting older. Mentally, they locked you in at eight, thirteen, nineteen—whatever age you were when they could no longer face the fact that you were growing up and growing away from them. Tell them you're thirty-five, and they blot it out with reminiscences about your first tricycle, your first report card, the big vacation the whole family took when you were in seventh grade, and...well, you get the picture.

And speaking of pictures, take a look around your parents' house. Are there pictures of you? Sure—but from what time period? Your high school graduation or, at the latest, your college graduation? There you are, up on the wall or on top of the TV, frozen in time, with a ridiculous hairdo and an "I'm eighteen and aren't I cool" look on your face—just the way your parents are determined to remember you.

Don't bother trying to bring the picture gallery up to date. If you give your parents a copy of the publicity photo you had taken when you were promoted, they'll say, "How nice," tack it on the refrigerator with a slice-of-lemon magnet for a week or two, then put it away in a drawer somewhere—leaving that faded reminder of your adolescent glory on prominent display. Still their baby. Still the fresh-faced kid just stepping into the real world to seek fame and fortune. Never mind that you have been working for ten years, have gotten married, had two kids, gotten divorced, and are thinking about changing careers (having already had at least one career to change from).

"Well," your parents will say in their defense, "nobody wants to have *old* children, do they?"

When you were fifteen, they were, at worst, middle-aged. But if you're thirty-five, they're ancient. Your being middle-aged puts them one breath away from a respirator—and, understandably, they can't bear to think about it.

Besides, they had years to get into the habit of being parents, and some of them not only got used to it, they got downright dependent on it. They want to be needed, they want to be loved, they want the patter of little feet or the thud of smelly sneakers around the house. They want their family back.

HOW TO COPE WITH THE PERPETUAL PARENT

1. Treat your parents like adults, not like parents. Use the same courtesy, diplomacy, and restraint you'd use in dealing with a friend or co-worker.

2. Act like an adult around your parents. Any childish behavior gives your parents an opportunity to baby you.

3. Politely ask your parents to stop treating you like a child.

4. When that doesn't work, you can disengage yourself from the Parents-Baby game.

5. Don't lose your temper.

Pretty simple, right? Easy for *me* to say, right? But it can be done. Let's see how to apply these rules to the top six Perpetual Parent types: the Fusser, the Worrier, the Amplifier, the Adviser, the Used-to-Be's, and the Family Mediator.

THE FUSSER

"Can I Get You a Cup of Coffee, Turn up the Heat, Do Your Laundry, Make a Sandwich for You...?"

You are sitting alone in your parents' living room, engrossed in the latest best seller. The hero, a San Francisco homicide detective, is searching for a fourteen-year-old girl who has been kidnapped by an escaped convict. An anonymous caller has provided a tip to the detective that the girl might be in one of the deserted warehouses near the wharf. It's dark, and the fog is so thick that the detective's flashlight beam barely reaches the ground. He shines the light on one of the old, weather-beaten doors, and sees that there's a new padlock holding it shut. Could this be the convict's hideout? Then, suddenly, with no warning whatsoever, out of the mist comes...

Your mother.

"Is it warm enough in here for you, dear? Let me get a blanket for your feet."

"No, thanks, Mom, it's plenty warm in here." She puts the blanket over your feet anyway, then leaves.

You scan down the page, looking for your place. Let's

see . . . anonymous caller, warehouse, flashlight beam . . . oh, yes, *He shined the light on one of the old, weather-beaten doors and saw that there was a new padlock . . .*

"I brought you a Coke, dear." Mom's back. "Would you like a sandwich with it?"

"No, thanks, Mom. We just had dinner half an hour ago."

"Oh." She leaves.

He shined the light on one of the old, weather-beaten doors and saw that . . .

"Well, here's a dish of peanuts and some pretzels"—she's back again—"just in case you get hungry."

"Yeah, great, Mom," you mutter, not looking up from your book.

He shined the light on one of the old, weather-beaten . . .

"It seems awfully dark in here, dear. I'd better turn that light up. You'll ruin your eyes." Your mother cranks up the lamp and tilts the shade so that 375 watts (where *do* your parents find these light bulbs?) are blazing down on the pages of your book.

You grit your teeth and wait for your eyes to adjust. Now, where were you? Okay, here it is: *He shined the light on one of the . . .*

Your mother plops herself down on the couch next to you and says, "Is that the new Joseph Wambaugh novel? No? Who wrote it? Is it any good? What's it about? Would your father enjoy it? Would I?"

Suddenly a kidnapping doesn't seem like such a bad idea. Maybe there's an escaped convict in the neighborhood who'd like to take your mother off your hands for a few days.

My Mother Loves Me

The Fusser (almost exclusively a mother syndrome) has a compulsive need to take care of you. She can't leave you alone. She strives to anticipate your every need and to answer it before you can open your mouth to ask. She brings you food, drink, sweaters, slippers, the newspaper. She'll fight you all the way from the refrigerator to the silverware drawer if you try to make your own midnight snack. She'll rip the clothes out of your hands if you try to do your own laundry. Any effort to help her around the house is met with "You should take it easy while you're here; you work too hard."

The Fusser insists that you let her "do" for you, and she won't take no for an answer.

All this attention is flattering—"Mom loves me so much she just can't do enough for me"—but it's also oppressive. Your mother treats you like a helpless child, because she wishes you still were one. She wants her baby back. She wants you completely dependent on her. She wants the unqualified affection and total adoration you used to give her when you were small.

How to Stop Her Compulsive Mothering

Since you probably have no desire to be either helpless or an infant—or to be stuck on the same sentence of your cop novel forever—you've got to put the brakes on Mom.

The best defense is to use your mother's desire to make you happy against her—disguised, of course, as your concern for *her* best interests. After the initial onslaught of blankets and peanuts, say:

"Mom, do you know what would make me *really* happy?"

"No, what?" she'll say, poised in the starting blocks for a run to the kitchen or the drugstore or the nearest Burger King.

"It would make me really happy if you would sit down and relax. You shouldn't be running around like this. Why don't you sit here, and I'll get *you* something to drink?"

With committed Fussers, this will only be a temporary fix. An hour later, when she starts in again, frown and say more firmly, "I'm serious, Mom, I feel as if I'm causing you a lot of extra work. I don't want you to wait on me; it makes me feel bad for putting you out."

Don't stop there, or you'll get a lecture on how she is not "put out" by taking care of her own children. Continue with: "And you don't want me to feel bad, do you?" The catch-22 of making you unhappy by trying to make you happy should get her to ease up.

"You'll Always Be My Baby—or Else"

On the other hand, it may make her mad, because you're ruining the Mommy-Baby game. She may say, "Well, it's too bad some people don't appreciate it when someone tries to do something nice for them." Or "That's what I get for trying to take care of you—who else but your mother would do this for you?" But the real message is "Stop acting like a grown-up and start acting like my child."

In this case, you're the one who should be mad, because playing mommy is more important to her than having a reasonable relationship with the adult you are now. She wants to deliver affection on *her* terms, whether you like it or not.

So if she gets in a snit because you don't want to be treated like a three-year-old, stand your ground. Don't give in and think, Oh, well, Mom's just trying to be nice, so I'll let her drive me crazy. Get to the heart of the problem. *Without* sounding annoyed, ask her, "Why are you treating me as if I'm helpless? It makes me think you would be happier if I were three years old again."

If that doesn't work, drop the ultimate threat on her— no baby to fuss over. Say:

"Don't you think it's time you stopped waiting on me hand and foot? My visits seem to throw you into a frenzy, and that makes me feel guilty. Maybe I should come less often or not come at all."

It May Never Have Occurred to Her...

In all fairness, some mothers don't know how to show affection except by babying you. They don't know you as an adult, so they don't know what you, as an adult, would like. So give your mother a few suggestions. Ask that she teach you how to make her famous biscuits, or hint around that she could baby-sit the kids while you and your spouse go out to dinner—yes, go out to dinner alone, with your mate, while you're staying at your parents' house. It's a radical thought, perhaps, but baby-sitting would be doing something for you the adult, not you the child.

You Can't Have It Both Ways

Make sure that you're not encouraging your parents to be Fussers. A large number of "children" keep acting like children long after they've turned twenty-one—and cause their parents to go right on acting like parents.

Don't let your parents do things for you that you wouldn't dream of letting a friend do—like washing your clothes, or changing your snow tires, or slipping you twenty dollars as you're walking out their front door.

That's being a child. That's whining, "Mo-o-om, I can't do all this by myself. You do some of it, okay?" And that's taking advantage of them.

You can't have it both ways. You can't say, "Mom, wash and iron my clothes, but don't zip up my jacket for me when I leave the house. Dad, change my snow tires, but don't tell me how to drive."

But they enjoy doing things for me, you may be thinking. It helps them feel as if they're still part of my life.

Darn right it does. It helps them pretend that you're still a child and they're still raising you.

Make up your mind: Are you an adult or a child?

THE WORRIER

*"You're Going to Get Mugged if You Keep Leaving Your
Office So Late at Night."*

Some parents were terrified the entire time you were
growing up that something awful would happen to you.
They feared you would be kidnapped by the neighborhood pervert, run over by a speeding mail truck, or fatally
infected by a piece of gum you found on the sidewalk.

Once you left home and were involved with dangerous
things like cars, airplanes, and your own apartment, your
parents were convinced your life was going to end at any
moment.

One mother nearly fainted when her only son and her
only daughter left town, on *airplanes,* on the *same day,* for
business trips. It was the ultimate potential disaster: both
her children reduced to flaming debris by a midair colli-
sion between their respective airplanes. She was certain
she'd never see either one of them alive again. She de-
manded that they call, first when they got to the airport,
and then when they reached their hotels. Even if they
made it that far, she was sure they'd be killed in simultane-
ous taxicab accidents on the way to their first meetings in
the morning.

Worriers don't understand that a parent's real purpose
in life is to prepare children to fend for themselves when
they grow up—to be self-sufficient, to be contributing
members of their communities, and not to be taken advantage of. No, Worriers think their purpose is to *protect* children from the real world: make sure that they are never in
danger, that their feelings never get hurt, and that they sail
through life happy and problem-free.

Too bad it doesn't work that way.

Too Much You

Worriers all suffer from the same problem: You, their child, are too important to them. Worriers focus exclusively on you, because they don't have anything else to think about. They never considered what they would do when you left the nest—or, more accurately, *fled* the nest, looking for someplace less smothering (which, you'll note, is a variation of the word *mother*). They were devastated when you left home and traded them in on a career, a marriage, or a new home in a new city.

Don't Get Into a Debate

The worst thing you can do with Worriers is argue with them. If you try to rationalize their fears away, you'll end up in a conversation like this:

THE WORRIER: Call me the minute you get there.

YOU: Don't worry, nothing's going to happen to me.

THE WORRIER: What do you mean? *Anything* could happen. Your plane could crash; you could get robbed; your hotel room could be broken into. Why, when Norma Coulter's son went to New York on business, everything he owned was stolen right out of his hotel room. If he'd been in the room at the time, he could have been shot, knifed, beaten up. . . .

YOU: But I'm not going to New York City; I'm going to Buffalo.

THE WORRIER: That's almost as bad. With the wind off the lake this time of year, you could get pneumonia. Are you taking your winter coat and an extra sweater?

YOU: I haven't had a cold in years, let alone pneumonia. I'm not going to get sick in Buffalo.

THE WORRIER: If you haven't had a cold for years, you're due for one. I know you won't take care of yourself, and by the time you get back you'll probably have to be hospitalized.

You can't win. There isn't a rational, logical argument in the world that can convince your parents you'll be all right —because this is not a rational, logical fear. Your parents are fearful for you, but they're even more terrified for themselves.

As one mother told her son, "If anything happens to you, I will have no reason to live."

Out-Worry Them

The best approach with Worriers is to show them how inappropriate their fears are by good-naturedly escalating those fears to the point of ridiculousness.

When a Worrier says something like:

> "Doris Abrahms's daughter had an accident this morning. Her car hit a telephone pole because one of her tires blew out. All day long I've had horrible visions in my mind of the same thing happening to you. I was afraid that if I didn't call and remind you to check your tires, something might happen, and then I'd never forgive myself."

Resist the temptation to:

1. Tell the Worrier to stop nagging you (after all, you're not seventeen anymore) or
2. Give the Worrier an in-depth account of your elaborate car-maintenance routines, which consistently exceed the recommendations of the manufacturer, Ralph Nader, and *Consumer Reports*.

Instead, show how inappropriate these fears are by exaggerating them. Do it in a friendly, "I'm teasing you because I like you" tone (parents take their neuroses seriously, so don't offend them).

> "I'd better leave work right now and head for the tire store. I'll also have my exhaust system overhauled so I don't get

overcome by carbon monoxide fumes. And I'll have my radiator replaced so the car doesn't overheat and blow up on me. Oh, hell, you're right—I'm going to have to buy a new car!"

Mention the Cost of Doing It Their Way

You can also point out the consequences of succumbing to their fears:

- "Do you want me to tell my boss I won't go on this business trip? I'll probably lose my job, or never again be considered for a promotion, but at least you won't have to worry."

- "You want me to move to a nicer neighborhood? I'll be glad to, but which would you prefer I do in order to afford the rent: stop eating or stop paying my utility bills?"

- "You want me to turn down this job offer because I'll have to move one hundred miles away? Okay, but they were going to pay me four hundred dollars more a month, so it will cost me almost five thousand dollars a year to keep you happy. Is that what you want?"

Drop Out of the Game

If those techniques don't work, just disengage. Refuse to participate in the "My children are the center of my universe" game.

If you go out of town, tell them nicely that you won't be calling. Don't make excuses, because excuses just raise the frenzy level. "I barely have time to make it from the airport to my first meeting" will only lead to an argument: "Do you mean to tell me that you can't find two minutes to pick up a phone when you know how worried I am?"

Take a hard line and say, "No, I'm not going to call you from the airport. I'll talk to you when I get back."

Of course, no self-respecting Worrier is going to take that kind of rejection lying down. The Worrier is not going to say, "You're right, I'm being silly. Have a good time—I'll see you next week." No, Worriers will tell you that they won't be able to sleep at night, that they won't have a moment's peace until they know you're safe, and that they can't understand how you could be so inconsiderate of them.

Because they're addicts. They are addicted to worrying. And you need to stop feeding their habit. Say, "Sorry, but I'm not going to call. I'll be fine, and so will you." Then add the most important part of the conversation: "Goodbye."

Teach your parents that when they begin the compulsive worrying routine, you disappear. You hang up or you leave. When they call and say, "You didn't answer your phone all weekend. I was afraid you'd been mugged by a drug-crazed junkie in an alley somewhere"—all they get from you is (1) an assurance that you're all right, and (2) a dial tone.

The Give-Me-Attention Ploy

Remember that obsessive concern with your safety is a way of getting attention. Your parents are saying, "I'm lonely and nobody's talking to me. But you're my child and I know you'll talk to me if I act upset." They want you to fill the void.

Sorry, but that's not your job. Your parents can find something else besides you to occupy their time—but they won't do that until you stop allowing yourself to be the main attraction.

"Honesty Is the Best Policy"

But your poor parents—they're so concerned, right?

Every adult child at some point feels the need to protect his or her parents. You don't want your parents to know that your marriage is in trouble, so when Mom asks how things are, you lie and say, "Never better." You don't want to admit that you were out getting drunk last night, so when Dad calls and says, "Where were you last night?" you lie and say you were walking the dog (even if you don't have a dog). When your parents come to visit, your "significant other" moves in with a friend so your parents won't find out you're living in sin.

Adult children who are otherwise honest people who pride themselves on their integrity will lie through their teeth to their parents. Why? Because they don't think their parents can take the truth. They are convinced that these little white lies are necessary to protect their fragile parents.

Don't be so patronizing. Your parents aren't nearly as fragile as you think. They've survived for decades without your protection, and they will somehow manage to go on living after you divulge the awful truth about where you were last night.

I'm not saying you should tell your parents everything, because there are some things they won't be able to handle. I don't mean hang-gliding or believing in socialized medicine, I mean being a drug dealer or a terrorist. But other than those sorts of touchy subjects, there's no reason to lie.

Your parents don't need to be protected—they're much more resilient than you think.

Be Yourself

Most adult children take the easy way out. "I only see my parents a couple of weeks a year," they say. "I can pretend to be what they want for that short period of time." That's true, but maybe you'd want to see them more often—and *enjoy* seeing them more often—if you didn't feel required to give an Academy Award–winning performance every time they show up.

Louise is thirty years old and a middle manager with a major telephone company. She doesn't mind visiting her parents except that she spends a great deal of time driving back and forth to the local 7–11. Why? Because she smokes, and she's afraid her mother will find out. So she drives to the 7–11, sits in the parking lot, has a cigarette, then drives home.

"For as long as I can remember, my mother has complained about smoking," Louise said. "She goes on and on about what a filthy habit it is, that nobody in our family smokes, and how glad she is that I never started doing something as nasty as that. What am I supposed to do? Ask her for a light the minute I walk in the door?"

Sarah is a hard-driving businesswoman, which her elderly father disapproves of, because he doesn't think it's ladylike behavior. So when he comes to visit—which, fortunately for Sarah, is only once or twice a year—Sarah plays the Little Working Girl for him. She comes home at five o'clock every day, instead of her usual seven or eight o'clock. She doesn't talk about how she got one of her suppliers to cut his price 15 percent, or how she outmaneuvered the competition to land a major account. She says she's just dabbling in the business world—just enough to support herself.

And by the time her father goes home, she's climbing the walls.

Pretending to be something you're not puts a staggering amount of tension into your relationship with your parents. Stop being a phony, and stop lying to your parents. Tell them who you really are.

Sure, there may be some screaming, possibly some begging, and certainly some lecturing. But that's all right— they are entitled to their opinions. And then you're entitled to tell them that (1) you have seriously considered their advice, even if they delivered it at 120 decibels, and (2) you've decided not to take it. And you're also entitled to tell them, also at 120 decibels if necessary, not to bring it up again.

It's important to act like an adult around your parents, but it's even more important to act like the adult *you really are*, not the one your parents want/expect/demand you should be.

THE AMPLIFIER

"You're Getting Married? I've Never Been So Happy! You're Also Moving to Anchorage? I'm Going to Kill Myself!"

Some parents—the Amplifiers—overidentify with you. Your successes are their greatest joys. Your defeats are their biggest disasters. They feel your every emotion more acutely than you feel it yourself.

Amplifiers are great to have around when good things happen, because you have your own unbridled cheering section. But they're not so great when events don't go your way, because instead of providing support, Amplifiers add to your misery. Problems throw them into a state of panic.

> **YOU** (CONCERNED): We've had another financial setback at work. According to the grapevine, they may start laying people off.

What you want to hear is:

> **A NORMAL PERSON'S REACTION:** That doesn't sound good, but I'll tell you something. I was laid off myself about five years ago, and it turned out to be the best thing that ever happened to me. I wouldn't be in the great job I'm in now if I hadn't been literally thrown out of my old one. So try not to worry about it. With your talent, you'll have no trouble finding not only a new job, but a better job.

Instead, what you get is:

THE AMPLIFIER (HORRIFIED): You're kidding! What are you going to do? Do you have any idea how tight the job market is right now? *Nobody's* hiring.

Even if you don't get laid off, and you're with that same company for the next ten years, your parents will keep asking, "How's your job? Has there been any more talk of layoffs? Don't you think you ought to look for another job?"

Does This Sound Familiar?

Amplifiers are what Worriers turn into when something actually does go wrong. As with Worriers, your best bet is to tell them to lighten up.

"Wait a minute, folks, I'm not ready for the bread line and the soup kitchen yet. All I said was that times were a little tough at work. Don't put me in the poorhouse before it's really necessary."

If that doesn't work, disengage yourself. Amplifiers, like Worriers, want you to participate in their hysteria—don't do it.

When It's Serious, Get Serious

When the problem is major, an Amplifier's overreaction can be a tremendous burden.

When Joan had a miscarriage, her Amplifier mother was inconsolable. "I don't understand how this could happen," her mother wailed. "There's never been another miscarriage in the family—on either your father's side or mine. Were you smoking or drinking while you were pregnant? Was it some drug you took in college? Oh, I can't believe this has happened to us. I cry every time I look at the baby clothes we bought. How will you ever have the courage to get pregnant again?"

Don't feel you need to carry both your burden and the one your parents are creating. Have a serious talk with them.

"I know you're upset, but this didn't happen to you. It happened to me. And I can't handle emotionally supporting both of us. Right now I need *you* to help *me*. Can you do that?"

If they can't, let them off the hook. Some parents can't handle their own problems, let alone yours. If they can't be supportive, explain as nicely as you can that because you don't have enough sympathy to go around for everybody, you're going to cut the conversation short, and that you'll talk to them when you all feel better.

THE ADVISER

"You Can't Live Your Life like That. You Should..."

The Advisers have a better way for you to do everything, and they can't wait to tell you about it.

- "You should pay more attention to your children. They act as if they're starved for affection."
- "You'd sound a lot more dignified if you stopped saying 'you know' at the end of every sentence."
- "You should lay off the sweets. I swear you've gained twenty pounds since the last time you were here."

Your parents deliver this nonstop stream of advice in the form of:

1. Direct assaults, like the statements above.
2. A third party: "Mom's worried about your weight."

3. Subtle hints, like "That sweater didn't used to be so tight on you. Did it shrink?"

4. Air mail: "Enclosed is an article about a woman in Omaha who lost 213 pounds in twelve days."

It makes you want to kill them.

The Omnipotent Parent

Sometime around the end of World War II, the so-called child-rearing experts decided that parents had unlimited power. They said to parents (mothers, in particular), "*You* determine whether your child will grow up to be a warm, wonderful, well-adjusted human being—or a neurotic basket case. What you do, or don't do, will mark this kid for life."

While that basic philosophy is correct (children who are loved and cared for usually turn out better than children who are abused and neglected), it got blown way out of proportion. Parents were told, and believed, that everything they did would have long-term effects. Like the trajectory of an arrow, the most minute error at the outset would mean a major miss later on.

So you—their child—stopped being a human being and started being a project.

"How did your kids turn out?" people asked (and still ask) your parents, as if you were a recipe for a delicate French pastry or a complicated macrame design.

Your parents take credit for everything you do right and get the blame for everything you do wrong. If you are the most successful broker on Wall Street, it's because they raised you right. If you're unemployed because the steel industry collapsed, they ask, "What did *we* do wrong?"

The quest to make you perfect continues to this day. In the true tradition of "a parent's work is never done," they never stop checking on you. They never stop molding you and shaping you and guiding you. Just a little fine-tuning here, a slight touch-up there, and maybe then you'll be done—their flawless, incomparable child who reflects, of course, their flawless, incomparable child-raising abilities.

How to Get Off the Project List

Never agree with Advisers' advice. It only encourages them. They'll say, "You agree with me about your weight? Well, then, what about your hair? You'd look so much better with your hair shorter. You agree? Then what about those clothes you're wearing? That jogging suit looks like a pair of pajamas. You agree? Well, what about...?"

There is no end.

It's also a bad idea to patronize Advisers, to say, "Yes, yes, I know I should do something about that," and then go on your merry way and ignore their advice. Because while you're being conciliatory and saying, "You're right, Mom, I really do need to lose twenty pounds; I'll have to cut back on the sweets," your mother is thinking, "I've told this fat slob eight thousand times that she needs to lose weight, and she keeps saying she's going to do something about it, but she never does. Why doesn't this kid pay attention?"

Of course, you can't *dis*agree with them, because their advice usually has some truth in it: You *are* too fat, your children *don't* go to the best day-care center in the world, and your English *wouldn't* win any awards.

The only thing you can do is thank them for their advice, tell them you're not going to take it, and tell them to leave you alone. But bear in mind the following suggestions for doing it in a diplomatic fashion:

Concede that they might have a point. Don't give in to their assessment of the situation, but let them know you're listening by saying, "You *may* be right, but..."

Tell them, in no uncertain terms, that you don't plan to follow their advice. Don't hesitate, equivocate, or show weakness of any kind—or they'll be all over you. Just de-liver a firm "I don't plan to do anything about that."

Before they can ask why, tell them why. Some stock rea-sons to draw from:

"I don't have the time."

"I don't have the energy."

"I can't afford it."

"I don't feel like it."

But be prepared. Hard-core Advisers will perceive these as flimsy excuses and have an answer for all of them:

"You could make the time if you really wanted to."

"You should do the important things first, while you're still fresh."

"Your brother makes less than you do, and he always seems to be able to find the money for things like this."

"What kind of answer is 'I don't feel like it,' for crying out loud?"

Don't argue with them. Your parents are convinced in every fiber of their beings that where you're concerned, they know best. So don't try to change their minds. Just close the door on further discussion by saying, "I appreci-ate your concern, but it's not something I'm going to worry about right now. Let's talk about something else."

Don't let them wear you down. If they get stubborn on you, say firmly, but politely: "Why do you keep bringing this up?"

Don't get mad and say, "What's the matter with you? Don't you understand English? [Remember that one?] I'm trying to get it through your thick skull [or that one?] that I don't want to talk about this anymore."

If you get mad, you lose the battle. You become an ingrate who doesn't understand that your parents are only looking out for your best interests. Your father will be disgusted; your mother will start crying. You'll end up saying that you're sorry, that yes, you will work on your vocabulary, or yes, you will change day-care centers, or yes, you will go on a diet immediately after eating the 8,649-calorie dinner (including four kinds of desserts) that your mother just put on the table.

Maintain a calm, dignified, pleasant exterior (no matter how much effort that takes), and continue to remind them that you don't want to talk about it—now or ever—and that you would like them to drop it. Sooner or later, they will.

THE USED-TO-BE'S

"You've Always Been Timid, Even When You Were in High School."

A long time ago, your Used-to-Be parents made a decision about what kind of person you were. For ease of handling, they condensed your personality down into a few traits and slapped a label on it: This kid is overly aggressive, terribly shy, the class clown, a bookworm, or the neighborhood bully.

Having gotten that judgment out of the way, they never reconsidered it. If you were a jerk at eighteen, they think you're a jerk today. If you were the most responsible kid on your eighth-grade softball team, then responsibility is one of your hallmark traits still. You were the child prodigy, the bumbling screw-up, or the James Dean type of sullen adolescent—and to your parents, you still are.

You Used-to-Be Such an Angel

Guaranteed to ruin your day is your parents saying how your life has been a long downhill slide since you peaked in your adolescent years—that it's too bad you never lived up to your potential. Your parents fondly remember back when you used to get really good grades, have the most friends, or be the best-dressed kid in school, and they mention in wistful tones that they don't know what happened to you.

What they mean is that they want you to have a more successful career, get along better with your neighbors, or buy a nicer wardrobe. This is just advice in disguise, so handle these folks just like you handle Advisers: Thanks, but no thanks.

Then make *them* feel guilty for being so critical by saying, "You sound disappointed in me. Didn't I live up to your expectations?"

You can't drop your parents the way you'd drop friends who were constantly disappointed in you—but you can threaten to, if they don't quit picking on you:

> "I'm sorry I've let you down so badly. Maybe you'd prefer I didn't come around so often? If not, maybe you'd like to stop asking, 'What happened?' "

Don't let them make *you* feel guilty. You don't need to live up to anybody's expectations of you, except your own.

You Used-to-Be Such a Bum

If your reputation was less than sterling as a child, it's hard to get credit for maturing.

> When Ned was in high school and college, he was always borrowing money, bumming cigarettes, getting someone else to drive and pay for the gas. He never kicked in his share. As he got older, he got over that unfortunate tendency, but he could never convince his parents that he had changed. When Ned went into business with a friend of his from college, his mother anxiously took him aside.

"Are you sure you're paying your half of the office expenses?" she wanted to know. "Larry's a nice boy, and I don't
want you taking advantage of him."

Accustomed to this line of questioning, Ned said wearily,
"Yes, Mother, I'm paying for half of everything."

"Even the rent? What about the utilities? What about sala-
ries? I don't want you to run off and leave Larry with a pile of
bills."

If your parents' low opinion of you has carried over
from your wild and crazy youth, it may take some work to
change their minds. Here's the strategy to use.

Accept their version of how you Used-to-Be. You can't
change anyone's mind about what the past was like.

Ask them to describe what you are like today. Accentuate
the positive here. Don't ask what makes them think you're
still *ir*responsible, because they'll come up with something:
"What about last week when you went to the grocery store
for us and forgot to buy your father's foot powder? Or last
year when you didn't call on Mother's Day?" They keep
track of these things.

Instead, ask what you've done that shows you've im-
proved.

Your conversation should go something like this:

YOU: I admit I was a little irresponsible (okay, a lot irresponsible) when I was in college.

YOUR PARENTS: No kidding. We couldn't believe it when you
cashed in your tuition check and went to Las Vegas.

YOU (TRYING TO ACT AMUSED): Yeah, it's hard to believe I
used to be that way. Thank goodness those days are over.

THEM: They're over?

YOU: Aren't they? Have I pulled anything like the Las Vegas
caper in the past ten years?

THEM: No, of course not, but when you were in college, you
Used-to-Be—

YOU: Am I still in college?

THEM: No, but—

YOU: Then why do you think I'm still that way? Don't you think it's possible I might have changed?

THEM: Well, maybe. You do seem to be more stable these days.

YOU: Then tell me what I'm like today.

THEM: Okay, okay, we'll stop mentioning Las Vegas.

YOU: I'm serious. Give me some examples of my fine-upstanding-citizen behavior.

THEM (SIGHING AND WONDERING WHAT HAPPENED TO THE KID WHO USED TO SAY, "JUST GIVE ME A BREAK, WILL YOU?" WHEN THE LAS VEGAS CAPER CAME UP): Let's see.... you've held down the same job for the past seven years. And you paid back that loan we gave you for your condo. Actually, you paid it back ahead of time, which was nice. And your marriage seems to be working out fine. Well, now that you mention it, maybe we have been under-estimating you.

If that doesn't work, and your parents continue with nostalgic Used-to-Be's that put you in an unfavorable light, ask why they keep bringing it up—Do they wish you were still that way (and still their crazy kid)? Or are they just trying to hurt your feelings?

Make Sure You're Not *What You Used-to-Be*

Before you confront your parents about their outdated opinions, make sure you don't become that bad old self when you're around them. If Ned is still "borrowing" cigarettes from his father and spare change from his mother, his parents have every right to treat him like a leech.

Returning "home" as an adult and immersing yourself in the old family environment can trigger your old behavior —without your even realizing it.

One woman told this story:

"I had been dating Randy for about six months when he decided it was time for me to meet his parents. We flew to

California to stay with them for a few days, and I got the shock of my life. Randy's normally gregarious, outspoken personality vanished. He wouldn't speak to his parents unless it was absolutely necessary, and when he did speak, he was sarcastic and insulting. If they walked into a room, he'd walk out. When I asked him what in the world was going on, he told me to mind my own business.

"I couldn't figure it out. His parents seemed like perfectly nice people to me, but he was rotten to them."

Whenever Randy is with his parents, it's a time warp back into his surly past. Even the presence of his adult girl-friend isn't enough to overcome his habit of acting like a brooding teenager around his folks.

It's no wonder they don't think he's changed.

Do *you* turn into some kind of monster when you're with your parents? Are you consistently sullen around them—or argumentative or sarcastic or defensive?

If so, maybe *you* are the reason you and your parents don't get along.

What Did Your Parents Used-to-Be?

In the interests of good relations, make sure *you* aren't reacting to conditions that no longer exist:

Clark, a thirty-three-year-old construction worker, automatically goes on the defensive when he's with his father—often even *before* he's with his father. His wife, Julie, said, "Clark and I seem to be running about fifteen minutes behind the rest of the world. We're always late. His parents know that and usually don't say anything, but when we're rushing around getting ready to go to his parents' house, Clark starts anticipating trouble from his father. He'll say, 'If the old man says anything about our being late, I'm going to tell him off. Who is he to give me a hard time, anyway? I get sick of his complaining about everything.'

And we haven't even left the house yet! When we get there,

his father doesn't say a word about our being late, and it takes half an hour for Clark to calm down."

Clark's father has gotten used to his son's chronic lateness, but Clark hasn't noticed. He still acts as if it's the bad old days when he was a teenager and got yelled at whenever he wasn't exactly on time.

Hey, Clark, times have changed.

THE FAMILY MEDIATOR
"If You'd Just Try, I Know You Kids Could Get Along Better."

Screaming, arguing, and even fistfighting between brothers and sisters is a standard part of family life. Mom arbitrates these battles, occasionally calling in Dad if the yelling escalates into furniture breaking. In the old days, good relations between the children, or at least some level of mutual tolerance, was a very high priority, since it meant Mom and Dad could sit and talk in their own living room, without toy guns and Barbie dolls whistling past their ears.

Today the children live in separate houses, probably in separate cities, and they no longer fight over who used whose bath towel and who borrowed whose jacket. Sisters no longer terrorize little brothers for talking to their dopey junior high school buddies on the phone when the fabulous Tommy might be trying to call. Brothers are no longer outraged that baby sisters want to tag along when "the guys" are hanging out in the neighborhood. There's no more disgusted sighing, name-calling, or door slamming.

But that doesn't deter Mom from her role as Manager of Family Relations. You still hear:

- "Why don't you let your sister move in with you? I know you've only got a studio apartment, but it would be just for a few months until she gets settled. She hasn't been as lucky as you, you know."

- "Your brother says you haven't paid him back the money you borrowed from him three weeks ago. He asked me not to say anything, but somebody's got to speak up for him— he's too nice to say anything himself."

- "After all the work your brother put in—free of charge, I might add—on your basement, you couldn't help him get his car started yesterday? I know you were on your way to a job interview, but couldn't you spare an extra ten minutes to help your brother?"

It Doesn't Matter Who's Right

Mom wants everybody to get along. At the first sign of trouble, she intervenes to enforce the peace. Because she can't spank you or send you to your room anymore, she uses guilt to get you to behave.

- Death is a major bludgeoning tool: "When your father and I are gone, you and your sister will have only each other. I couldn't go to my grave in peace knowing that you two were fighting."

- Family holidays are a biggy: "What about Thanksgiving and Christmas? If you and your brother aren't speaking, everything will be ruined."

- The "underprivileged sibling" rule is invoked on a regular basis: "You are more successful, better-looking, richer, smarter, or more famous than your brothers and sisters, so you give a little. They've suffered enough." Remember, Mom always roots for the underdog. (If you're the underprivileged sibling, you get to hear how much more successful, better-looking, richer, smarter, and more famous your brothers and sisters are—and that's its own punishment.)

You can't reason with the Family Mediator. Your mother will never believe that you couldn't have helped out just this one last time, that a little bit of extra effort on your part wouldn't have been too much to ask, so don't try to defend yourself or claim that your brothers or sisters are taking advantage of you. She won't buy it.

>**MOM:** You know, you're really a bad brother. Freddy told me how you refused to help him move into his new house. Maybe you're not aware of how little money he makes, but he can't afford professional movers like some people can.
>
>**YOU** (ALSO KNOWN AS "SOME PEOPLE"): Did he also tell you that he wanted me to come over at 3:00 A.M., when he got off shift, to start moving? Did he tell you that we had plans to go to the mountains that weekend? Did he tell you he gave me all of four hours' notice? Bad brother? What about all the times I've loaned that little weasel my car because he doesn't take care of his? What about the time he and his wife and those three totally out-of-control children stayed at my house for seven weeks? What about...?
>
>**MOM:** I know he's had some problems, but that should make you even more willing to help him.

How to Get Yourself Out of Arbitration

Our concern here, of course, is not how you and your siblings get along, but what your mother is doing in the middle of it. There's nothing wrong with talking to your mother about a problem you're having with a brother or sister, since she's well acquainted with all the parties involved. The problem arises when she (1) brings it up if you don't want to talk about it or (2) starts blaming you or insisting you should give in "for the sake of the family."

Don't be swayed by guilt. Tell her, nicely, to butt out.

>**YOU:** Mom, I know you want everybody to get along, but this is between Freddy and me. We're adults now, and we've got to work this out ourselves.
>
>**MOM:** (PUZZLED BY THIS NEW CONCEPT): Work it out yourselves?
>
>**YOU:** Yes. If you take sides, you're going to make this problem worse. If you take my side, Freddy will be mad at you,

and if you take his side, I'll be mad at you. So why not stay out of it?

MOM: But it's my responsibility to see that you kids get along.

YOU: No, it isn't. Mom, I'm not going to let you mediate this fight, or browbeat me into making up with Freddy.

MOM: But Freddy asked me to talk to you about it.

YOU: That was a mistake on Freddy's part. I don't think you should let Freddy hide behind you. If he has a problem with me, he should tell me himself. Then he and I can work it out—without you. And, Mom? I don't want to talk about this anymore.

It helps, during moments of calm, to let your brothers and sisters know you aren't going to let Mom mediate your fights and that it won't do them any good to run to Mama.

And make sure *you* aren't the one who's running to Mama and asking her to intercede on your behalf.

4

The Users

WHILE SOME PARENTS can't bear to see their children grow up, others—the Users—couldn't wait. Because once you hit adulthood, it was time to collect on their investment. "After all we've done for you," User parents say, "you owe us."

And they mean it. You started running a tab at conception, and when you finally became an adult, they handed you the bill.

INVOICE

   To: You

 From: Your Parents

  Date: Your Twenty-first birthday

Terms: Payment Terms to be determined by Mom and Dad

Invoice for services rendered as follows:

- Difficult pregnancy, 1954
- Being driven crazy by crying baby, 1954–1955
- Being driven crazy by screaming toddler, 1955–1959

- Not being able to go anywhere without getting a baby-sitter, 1954–1966
- Spending every cent we had on clothes and food for you, 1954–1974
- Being scared to death you were going to die of the flu, 1961
- Chauffeuring you all over town, 1965–1970
- Letting you use our car, 1970–1972
- Paying higher insurance premiums because you wrecked our car, 1971–1972
- Giving you the down payment to buy your own car, 1973
- Meeting with your teachers because of your rotten behavior, 1968–1969
- Meeting with the police because of your rotten behavior, 1971
- Spending every cent we had on your college education, 1972–1977

Those are just the highlights, of course, but User parents lavished time, effort, money, and attention on you, and now it's your turn to lavish back.

For years, they had to do without—without vacations, new clothes, and freedom—because of you. But it was all worthwhile, because now you can give them what they have been waiting for all these years: your undivided devotion during their old age. That means they want:

- Unlimited phone calls and visits.
- Unrestricted access to their grandchildren.
- Someone (you) to fix their leaky faucets and help them pick out new carpet.
- Someone (you) to make life better for them.

You are supposed to make them happy. You are supposed to solve their problems. You are supposed to improve their social standing, repair their car, give them something to rub their neighbors' noses in, and provide them with a lifetime of free furniture moving.

But that really isn't what you'd planned to do with your adult years, is it?

HOW TO COPE WITH USERS

Dealing with Users is simple—at least on paper.

1. Quit trying so hard to make your parents happy.
2. Stop letting them walk all over you.
3. Make what's best for *you* a higher priority than what's best for your parents.

Now let's see how to put those deceptively simple principles into practice with the Recruiter, the Pusher, the Weakling, and the Buddy.

THE RECRUITER
"I Know You're Busy, but It Would Be Such a Help if You Could Stop by and Paint Our Garage."

To some parents, you're a source of free labor: free housesitting, free decorating assistance, or free lawn service. One mechanically inclined son said, "I see my parents only on special occasions—Thanksgiving, Christmas, and whenever they need something fixed."

The Recruiters, with one eye on their bank account and one eye on the "You owe us" account, feel no remorse whatsoever about calling and "requesting" that you hustle on over to their house and do some work. Why pay somebody else to do it, when you'll do it for free?

When Ralph's parents got divorced, he, being the only son in the family, helped his father move into an apartment. Six months later, Ralph's mother decided that she didn't like living in that big house alone, so Ralph, being the only son in the family, helped *her* move into an apartment.

Ralph's father remarried eight months after that, and Ralph was called in to help him move into a bigger apartment. Then Ralph's mother decided she wanted to live as far away from Ralph's dad and his new bride as possible, so Ralph helped her move to an apartment on the opposite side of town.

A weary Ralph said, "In the last year and a half, I've moved more furniture than Allied Van Lines. And all for the low, low price of a couple of pizzas and all the Pepsi I could drink."

You Get What You Pay For

Rarely, of course, do you provide these services in a completely satisfactory fashion, but your parents can tolerate that, as long as you (or you and your spouse) devote all of your time and energy to taking care of their needs.

Sandra's mother mentioned repeatedly how nice it would be if Sandra's husband, Gary, would come over and take a look at their furnace—it had been making such strange noises lately. So Gary spent one whole Saturday afternoon working on it.

Then all Sandra heard was "I don't know, ever since Gary worked on the furnace, it's been putting out a funny odor. Don't say anything to Gary, because we wouldn't want to hurt his feelings, but do you think there might be a gas leak? I've been feeling awfully dizzy lately. I don't mean to criticize, you know, because it certainly was nice of him to spend all that time working on it—but do you think he might have broken something?"

Sandra said, "Mom, if you think something's wrong, hire a professional to come out and look at it."

"No, no," her mother assured her, "there's no reason to call somebody else when Gary can work on it."

Providing all these services may be an inconvenience, a lot of work, and generally a pain in the neck, but that gets you no sympathy from Recruiters. Raising you was also inconvenient, a lot of work, and generally a pain in the neck, but *they* survived it, didn't they? So when they whistle, you'd better jump.

Roger's dad, who owns a construction company, wasn't too happy when Roger became a barber. (Although Roger's dad thought "sissy hairdresser" was a more accurate description of what Roger did. He worked in a fancy salon, and he even cut *women's* hair now and then.) But at least it meant free haircuts for the old man. Whenever he wanted one, he'd call Roger at the shop and say, "I'll be over in an hour." At first, Roger didn't have many customers and he could always fit his father in. But as he got busier, that became more difficult.

One Saturday afternoon Roger's dad called and announced, "I'll be over at two-thirty." But instead of responding with his usual "Fine, come on by," Roger said, "Dad, I'm booked solid today. Saturday is always a busy day. How about if we do it Tuesday?"

Roger's dad skipped *annoyed*, glossed over *mad*, and went straight to *apoplectic*. "So Mr. Big Shot doesn't have time for his father anymore, huh? You had plenty of time for me when you needed money for barber college. Well, I'm not going to make a goddamn appointment to see my own son. I'll get a haircut somewhere else." And he slammed down the phone.

How's that for a big-time "I did for you, now you'd better do for me—or else" statement.

The Fictional "You Owe Me" Account

You may not believe this, but you don't have to jump every time your parents whistle. You are not an indentured servant, and you are not obligated to work off your "debt."

The big news is that you don't have a debt. The "You

owe me" account doesn't exist. It never did. The only place it exists is in your parents' minds; they invented it, and they perpetuate it. It's a fictional bill that you don't have to pay.

"But," you protest, "my parents have done so much for me. They raised me, put a roof over my head, fed me, and took care of me. I never wanted for anything."

What, I ask you in return, were they supposed to do—discard you in an alley, lock you in the basement until you were sixteen, or sell you to gypsies?

Let's look at this objectively. Who decided to have a baby, and who decided to raise you instead of putting you up for adoption? Your parents. Who decided to forgo a career to stay home and make sure Donna Reed didn't put her to shame? Your mother. Who decided to stay with the same job for twenty-five years to support his family? Your father.

You weren't involved. Your parents decided all by themselves, and it's not your responsibility to make restitution if they don't like the consequences of those decisions.

You owe your parents two, and only two, things:

1. To take care of yourself and not be a burden to them.
2. To make sure they are taken care of—which is not the same as personally taking care of them yourself—when they are no longer able to care for themselves.

That's it. That's all. You don't owe it to them to entertain them, to become a veterinarian just like Dad, or to wash their kitchen floor—no matter what they might tell you.

Pressure Comes from Within

Nobody can pressure you unless you allow it. If your next-door neighbor asks you to come over and shovel the snow out of his driveway, you can readily tell him—with no hesitation, guilt, or remorse whatsoever—to take a flying leap. You can say, "Sorry, pal, I'm on my way to the movies."

But the same request from your parents is a whole different scenario.

"Sweetheart," your mother says, sounding helpless, "if it wouldn't be too much trouble, do you think you might come over this afternoon and shovel our driveway? We can't even get the garage door open."

Uh-oh. You don't want to, but what if you say no? They'll do it themselves. Your mother might fall and break her hip, and the phones might be out of order because of the heavy snow, and Dad wouldn't be able to get the garage door open, and even if he could, he'd never get the car through the snow on the driveway, and Mom would lie in the car suffering, and if it was an open fracture, she might have ruptured an artery, and she'd bleed to death before Dad could trudge through the snow to a neighbor's house to call an ambulance, and once he got there, the neighbors might not be home, and...

"I'll be right over," you say. Your parents are right. You *are* the only person on the planet who can handle this emergency. Only you possess the snow-shoveling skills necessary to avert this potential disaster. And only you will charge them a fair and reasonable fee for this service: zero.

Say No

There is a marvelous little word in the English language that will cure any number of problems with your parents. It's *no*. Capital *N*, capital *O*, capital *NO*. No, I'm sorry. No, I can't. No, I don't have the time. No, I don't have the energy. No, I don't have the expertise. Sorry, no.

It works like a charm.

I know you've never done it before, but just for the sake of argument, let's say you get up the courage to say no to your parents. You decide there's another way to handle this snow crisis besides driving forty-five minutes across town in a blizzard. The conversation might go like this:

"Mom, I'm not going to drive anywhere in this weather."
"I know it's terrible out, dear, and I wouldn't dream of ask-

ing, except that if you don't come over, you father will go out
and shovel the driveway himself. In fact, he's waxing up the
shovel right now. I'm scared to death he'll have another heart
attack."

"Mom, why don't you give Robby down the block five bucks
to do it? He's sixteen—he'll do anything for money."

"*Five* dollars? For shoveling the driveway? That's absurd."
She sighs. "My arthritis isn't as bad today as it usually is. I
suppose I could do it myself."

Hold it right there. Before we go on, you need to realize
that the problem is not the snow that needs shoveling. The
problem is that Mom wants you to prove, by coming over
and shoveling the snow in their driveway yourself, that you
still love them and that you're still under their thumb.

Don't do it. If Dad's really going to shovel snow with a
weak heart, and your mother really won't try to stop him,
go around them. Call up Robby yourself, and promise him
five dollars to shovel their driveway.

When your parents try to stop him (which they will), tell
him to say he's already been paid. No self-respecting parent who even vaguely remembers the Depression will pass
up already-paid-for goods and services.

Then wait for your mother to call.

"That was very nice of you to have Robby shovel the driveway for us, dear. Although, for five dollars, I think he could
have done a much better job."

"Mom, can you get in and out of the driveway?"

"Yes, but—"

"Then Robby earned his five dollars."

Next time, let your folks call Robby. Or put Robby on a
retainer to do snow removal until April, and tell your parents it's their Christmas present.

But don't let your mother make you feel guilty.

"I know Robby tries hard, dear, but your father had to go out and help him."

"Mother, if you let Dad shovel snow, I can only assume that you're trying to kill him and collect his life insurance. If Robby didn't do a good job, there are at least six other teenage boys in your neighborhood who could handle it."

"Well, I still don't see why *you* couldn't have done it."

"Because I didn't want to. And don't tell me I'm an ungrateful child, because I'm not—and I've got a receipt for five dollars to prove it."

Snow shoveling may not be your particular problem, but active resistance and that little word *no* work every time.

Solve the Problem in Advance

To keep Recruiters from driving you to your emotional knees, preventive measures are called for.

Fortunately, Recruiters always give you plenty of warning that you're going to be pressed into service. They mention months in advance that they're going to clean out the shed behind the house—and, boy, are some of those boxes heavy. They talk about getting new furniture and wonder out loud where they're going to put the old stuff. They complain that the lawn mower isn't working quite right.

Our friend Roger knew his father's "no appointment needed" tactics would eventually cause a problem, but he did nothing about it. As soon as his clientele began to increase, Roger should have warned his father that he might not be able to take him on such short notice. Roger could have scheduled the appointment himself by saying, "You're about due for a haircut, aren't you, Dad? My schedule is pretty full now, so I thought I'd set up a time for you next week. How about four o'clock on Tuesday?"

Or Sandra, noticing that the "hint parade" had started, and knowing that nothing was ever done to her mother's satisfaction, could have told her mother: "I asked Gary about working on the furnace, Mom, but he says he doesn't know anything about furnaces like yours. He'd be glad to check around, though, and find someone else for you."

Recruiters are easier to combat if it's your spouse they're after. When Gary wasn't around, Sandra could have told her mother, "I can't seem to get Gary to relax anymore—it's work, work, work. I know you need the furnace looked at, but I'm trying to get him to take it easy. Could you get somebody else to do it this year? And, by the way, don't say anything about this to Gary. He'd be furious if he thought I was *un*volunteering him for this. You know how much he likes you two."

THE PUSHER

"What Do You Mean You Don't Want to Be a Doctor? Of Course You Want to Be a Doctor."

All parents think their children will be smarter, more successful, better looking, and happier than they are (otherwise, who would have kids?). While you were still womb-bound, your parents knew for a fact that you would one day be the president of the United States, the winner of the Nobel Peace prize, or the first junior high school student to become a millionaire.

Most parents get over these fantasies somewhere between the Terrible Twos and your struggle with calculus, but Pushers don't. They're still waiting for you to deliver the White House or a trip to Stockholm.

A Pusher Catalog

Pushers come in three heartwarming varieties:

Social Climbers want you to improve their standing in the world—or at least in their neighborhood. If you are an actor (working), author (published), professional football player, or rock 'n' roll star, it makes *them* more famous. If you are a doctor, lawyer, or the president of IBM, it makes *them* more respected. If you are rich, it makes them deliriously happy.

At the bare minimum, they expect you to do better than their friends' children, because—as psychologists have pointed out—if you are more successful, then they were better parents.

Standard Bearers have a tradition for you to live up to. They start sentences with "In this family, we have always" and finish them with phrases like "been lawyers," "had college degrees," or "given our children piano lessons."

You're expected to tow the family line.

Dreamers have a specific goal for you to achieve: the one they weren't able to achieve for themselves. They want you to be a sports hero, an actor, or the president of a *Fortune* 500 company. Dreamers are especially pushy if they believe having children was the reason they couldn't fulfill their own dream. You took it away; you can give it back.

"But We're Doing This for You"

Pushers try to convince you—and themselves—that everything they do is for your own good. Mothers, especially, are supposed to be selfless creatures: totally loving, completely giving, absolutely devoted, and interested only in what makes their children happy.

Right.

But back here in reality, "for your own good" often means for *their* own good.

One set of parents never failed to point out to their twenty-seven-year-old son, Dennis, how small his salary was as a newspaper reporter. "With all the hours you put in, it's criminal what they pay you. They're taking advantage of you," his parents would say. "Doesn't it bother you to make so little money and have to live in that run-down one-room apartment?" It certainly bothered them.

Even though Dennis loved the newspaper business, the constant nagging about his paycheck began to get to him. One day when his boss was yelling about a tight deadline, Dennis jumped up and said, "You don't pay me enough to take this crap," and walked out.

To his parents' delight, Dennis took a job as an insurance salesman. He now makes twice as much money, can afford a nice house and car, and his parents are ecstatic. But every morning it's an effort for Dennis to get out of bed, because he hates his job.

Phyllis, a computer analyst, became engaged to an English professor from a small college. Phyllis was happier than she had been in years, but when she called her mother with the good news, she heard nothing but silence. "What's the matter, Mom? Aren't you happy for me?"

"Of course I am, dear," her mother said, sounding sad. "It's just that I had hoped you'd end up with somebody like one of those executives you work with, somebody who makes seventy or eighty thousand dollars a year."

When you get pushed, prodded, hinted at, or ordered to do it their way, ask your parents, "Who is this for, you or me? Who does it really benefit, you or me?"

Don't be surprised when they answer, "Why, you, dear, of course. We're only looking out for your best interests."

"But if I'm not happy doing it your way," you might reply, "how can it be in my best interests?"

"Because you don't see the big picture. You don't realize how much this will benefit you later on. You don't have the perspective we do. Why, when you were in high school—"

"Am I still in high school?"

"No, but it's the same thing," they'll say.

"No, it isn't. I was sixteen years old then. I'm old enough now to know what I'm doing."

What Are You Afraid Of?

Anyone over the age of twenty-one who says, "I'd like to do this or that, but my parents would never get over it," is a coward. You're either afraid of your parents, or you're afraid to go after what you want in life, so you hide behind your parents' wishes.

You've got to be honest with your parents and tell them the truth.

> **THE PUSHER:** That promotion will really set you up for a shot at a vice presidency.
> **YOU:** I know, but I've decided to turn it down. I'm not spending enough time at home right now, and this promotion will mean even more traveling.
> **THE PUSHER** (AGHAST): You can't do that!
> **YOU:** Yes, I can. It's *my* career.
> **THE PUSHER:** You'll be sorry. You'll never get anywhere with this company if you pass up this chance to get ahead.
> **YOU:** I fully understand the risks, and I appreciate your concern. But I've spent a lot of time thinking about it, and turning it down is the right thing for me to do.

Pushers will try to rationalize what they view as your bizarre behavior. They'll say, "You're just tired," "You've been working too hard lately," or "The kids are wearing you down." And they'll advise you to "get away for a few days, and you'll feel better."

Take this for what it is: an insult to your ability to analyze a situation and make a competent decision about it. So give it to them straight. Don't apologize and don't change your mind. Tell them that you're going to live life *your* way.

You Versus Your Parents' Friends

And don't let yourself be abused by parents whose primary concern is what their friends will think.

After a quick rise through the company, Margo was promoted to sales manager. Back home, her parents were very proud, and they loved bragging to their friends about how well Margo was doing—especially since none of their friends' children were doing nearly as well.

But the big promotion didn't last. The aggressive management style Margo had used to get ahead didn't sit well with the sales force—most of whom had been with the company for years and were quite a bit older than Margo. Within six months, she was back in her old job.

Her parents were not only disappointed, they were embarrassed. "We told all our friends about your promotion," they said in dismay. "What are we going to tell them now?"

They gave it some thought and came up with this ingenious solution: "If anyone asks, we'll just say that you're still the sales manager. That way we won't have to explain why it didn't work out. Nobody around here will know the difference."

Margo deserves to be treated with more respect than that, and she has a right to demand better treatment.

THE WEAKLING

"I Don't Know What to Do. You'll Take Care of It for Me, Won't You?"

Defenseless and helpless in the face of the overpowering demands of life, Weaklings want you, their child, to rescue them. They cry out in the wilderness: "I can't," "I don't know how to," "I'm afraid to," and "Won't you handle it for me, please?"

Rarely are these tasks Herculean. Rarely does a parent say, "I'm on the way to the hospital to get the results of my biopsy, and the doctor says it doesn't look good. It would mean a great deal to me if you were there when I got the news."

No, these tasks are on the order of:

- "I can't balance my checkbook."
- "I don't know how to use a self-service pump."
- "I'm afraid to call the electric company about this $965 bill. Maybe it's something I did."

Weaklings take no pride in doing things for themselves or learning how to do something new. The only thing they enjoy is having you take care of them.

Weaklings are usually mothers, often widowed or divorced, but fathers can be just as bad. A man who built a three-room addition onto his house when his wife was alive often can't do a load of laundry when she's gone.

What all Weaklings want is attention, and they get it by acting helpless...sometimes real helpless.

Ellen's divorced mother was redecorating her bedroom in an attempt to chase out the old memories. She called Ellen one afternoon. "I've just been to the mall, and I bought new curtains, sheets, and bedspreads for the bedroom," she said. "Could you come over and help me get them out of the car and into the house?"

"They're in the car?" Ellen asked, confused.

"Yes. You wouldn't believe how much these bedspreads weigh."

"Then how did you get them into the car?"

"I carried them, of course. That's how I know how heavy they are."

"Mother, if you carried them to the car, why can't you carry them into the house?"

"*Because,*" her mother said, exasperated, "two sets of floor-length curtains, two sets of sheets and pillowcases, and two twin bedspreads must weigh over a hundred pounds."

"But you don't have to carry them in all at once, do you? Why don't you carry them in one at a time?" suggested Ellen. "Start with a set of pillowcases and work your way up to the bedspreads."

"Well, if you don't want to help me," her mother said indignantly, "why don't you just come out and say so?"

You don't mind when your ten-year-old daughter doesn't know how to operate the dishwasher, but when your sixty-year-old mother can't figure it out, it drives you crazy. You don't expect your third-grade son to know how to sew on a button or heat up a can of ravioli, but your sixty-five-year-old father?

You knew *you* were supposed to be self-sufficient when you grew up, but you expected your parents would be, too.

It's like Having More Children

Unless it's a result of illness or disability, treat these regressors to childhood the same way you'd treat your own children.

> **MOM:** I can't take my car to Midas. I wouldn't know what to say to them.
>
> **YOU** (VERY PATIENTLY): What do you think you should say to them?
>
> **MOM** (WORRIED): I don't know.
>
> **YOU:** What about telling them your muffler is making funny noises?
>
> **MOM** (PICTURING A DOZEN GREASE-LADEN BARBARIANS SCOWLING AT HER): But they'll want me to tell them what's wrong with it.
>
> **YOU:** No, they won't. Their job is to tell *you* what's wrong.
>
> **MOM:** But I've never taken a car in to be repaired before. They'll overcharge me. They'll sell me parts I don't need. They'll make me sit in a grimy waiting room all day.
>
> **YOU:** Mother, I don't know anything about cars, either, so unless you can find someone who does, you'll just have to go down there by yourself and take your chances. Believe me, the first time is always the hardest.

Your Parents Are Grown-Ups, Too

While your parents are begging you for help, remember: You are *not* responsible for taking care of parents who are really quite self-sufficient.

Bill's widowed mother had worked for several years in a kitchen wares store, and finally decided to open her own shop. Although it wasn't going to make her rich, sales were good enough to cover expenses and even show a small profit. Her late husband's pension plan more than took care of her personal needs.

Then Bill got a call from her. "If I didn't have to pay rent on my apartment," she said, "I could afford to put a better line of merchandise in, do some advertising, and really make this store go.

"Besides, since your father passed away, it's been so lonely. I can't tell you how much I hate living alone. And my health seems to be declining. I'm afraid I'll have a stroke or fall down and break my leg; it would be days before anyone found me."

Bill, an otherwise bright man, talked his wife into letting his mother move in with them. He felt he owed it to her. After all, hadn't she let him live with her for twenty years? In the interests of avoiding problems, the three of them sat down and drew up a set of rules: what area of the house Mom could use, what meals and cleaning she was responsible for, how much baby-sitting she would do, etc.

The day after she moved in, Mom threw her copy of the rules list in the trash can. She not only didn't do her share of housecleaning, she even refused to clean the room she was living in—poor health, she claimed. She complained to Bill's wife that Bill was too strict with the children and was destroying their initiative. She complained to Bill that his wife didn't like her and was rude to her when Bill was gone. She told the children that their parents were mean and selfish for not buying them the clothes and toys they wanted.

Within three months, Bill's mother was back in her own apartment, and nobody was speaking to anybody.

It is a law of nature that the more you help Weaklings, the weaker they become. If you let them, they will prey on you and your good intentions until you haven't got anything left for anybody else.

Your parents' childhood is over. They're adults, and you

should treat them like adults—whether they want you to or not.

Don't Turn Your Parents into Weaklings

If there's one thing worse than Weakling parents, it's adult children who try to turn their parents into Weaklings when those parents are perfectly capable of taking care of themselves.

Are you convinced that if you don't take care of these old people, no one else will? If your parents are senile, bedridden, or incontinent, you may be right. Otherwise, you may be having an attack of misguided benevolence. Because a sixty-five-year-old woman walks into the kitchen to get something, then can't remember what, doesn't mean that she should be institutionalized. (If that were the case, we should all be locked up.) If you tell your seventy-year-old father something and two hours later he's forgotten it, that's two hours longer than your fourteen-year-old son would remember it. Neither your father nor your son is coming down with Alzheimer's—they just aren't paying attention.

The first time your father asks, "What did you say?" don't march him down to the hearing-aid store. Don't pester your mother to put on a sweater so she won't catch pneumonia. Stop believing that if you don't take care of these old people, they're doomed.

Recently a nationally syndicated columnist printed a letter from a woman who said her parents' house was loaded with junk, and asked what she should do about it. There was no indication that the junk constituted a health hazard or a fire risk; it was just stuff her parents had accumulated over the years and refused to part with.

This columnist advised the daughter to clean everything out of the house and organize a yard sale to get rid of it. He said to arrange for Goodwill, or one of the other charitable organizations, to pick up all the unsold junk at the end of the day so her parents wouldn't be tempted—or able—to put it back in the house.

Strange advice, to say the least. I wondered how this columnist would feel if *his* kids invaded his home one day, removed all his "junk," sold it to strangers, and hauled away anything that was left. I bet he would be just tickled to death.

Your parents don't want to be treated like helpless children any more than you do. They have gotten by just fine for the past sixty or seventy years, thank you very much, and despite *your* desire to be in control, they don't need you to run their lives.

So lighten up, and mind your own business.

THE BUDDY

"You're My Best Friend."

Like Worriers and Weaklings, Buddies have a vacuum in their lives: not enough friends, hobbies, work, or love. But they figure you can take up the slack. They call you every day. They want to have lunch once a week, go shopping together, take vacations together, and be with you at every possible opportunity.

As one woman put it, "My mother wants me to go steady with her."

Why Can't We Be Friends?

Let's be honest with each other. If Mom and Dad were just two other people you worked with, went to the same church with, or lived down the block from, you probably wouldn't buddy around with them. You'd chat amiably when you happened to run into them. It's hard to be friends with people who are twenty, thirty, or forty years older and whose interests and attitudes are just too different.

Here you are, doing all the things they did years ago—getting married, raising kids, pursuing a career—and the temptation for them to play adviser is irresistible. They can't help bestowing upon you the benefit of all their years of experience. And they can't help bestowing it at every possible opportunity.

Stop Holding Your Parents Down

If you let yourself become your parents' best friend, you keep them from leading a normal life. With you to fill the void, there is no incentive for them to make friends their own age, get remarried, do volunteer work, get a job, or join a club.

With you, they don't have to be on their best behavior. They don't have to dress up, clean the house, or be polite. And they know you won't reject them—because, as they will remind you, you are their child and your attachment to them is permanent.

You're not helping them; you're stifling them.

How to Disengage Yourself

Don't pull the "Mirage" on your parents and just disappear. That's not fair, and it will hurt their feelings. Just be honest with them:

> "You are way too dependent on me. You need to have your own life with your own friends. You don't need to be hanging around with somebody twenty-five years younger than you, even if that somebody is me. Let's cut this back to once a week"—or once a month or once a day or whatever's appropriate.

That will start them wailing. They'll say that you are abandoning them, that you don't like them (no, that you *hate* them), that you have no respect for them, that you don't know how much they love you, that maybe you're up to something you don't want them to know about.

Tell them it's none of the above.

"You have nothing in your life besides me, and that's not good. What about joining that political committee Rosemary keeps bugging you to work on? What about the church group you used to go to? What about taking a class on home mainte-nance so you can fix the house up?"

Your parents will have 1,001 excuses why none of that is possible, but stick to your guns:

"Once a week, folks—or maybe less—until you stop mak-ing me carry the entire burden of your social life."

If your parents aren't well entrenched in the Buddy role, be ever vigilant for signs that they might be sliding into the role of best friend. As tactfully as possible, cut them off.

Donna, a television anchorwoman in Denver, was engaged to a military man stationed in San Antonio, and the wedding was to be held in her home town of Philadelphia. Because of the logistics involved, and Donna's heavy work schedule, her mother coordinated the arrangements from Wedding Central in Philly. Donna and her mother usually conferred once a day (three times a day while they were fighting about whether or not Donna would wear a veil).

After an unusual two days of noncommunication, Donna's mother called. "I haven't heard from you for *two days*. Are you all right?"

Smart enough to spot trouble when she saw it coming, Donna said, "You realize that all these phone calls are going to come to an end, don't you, Mom? We won't be able to do this after the wedding. I love you, but I'll have a husband and a job, and you and I will have to go back to just talking every couple of weeks."

Have You Set Your Parents Up?

Some adult children (not you, of course) are unable to cut their own umbilical cords; they cling to their parents when things aren't going well—and that sets their parents up to act like Buddies.

> When Connie's husband took a job in Arizona, it was the first time Connie had lived away from her hometown of Topeka, Kansas. She was homesick. She missed her friends; she missed her family. She had trouble finding a job and meeting people. To combat her loneliness, she started calling her mother. She called almost every day and she wrote every week. She invited her mother out for month-long visits, and she went back to Topeka to visit as often as she could.
>
> Her mother became indispensable.
>
> However, the new job didn't live up to expectations, and eighteen months later, Connie and her husband were back in Topeka. Connie soon got a job and fell back in with her old circle of friends. And soon she was complaining, "I can't get my mother to stop calling me and dropping by. She won't leave me alone. I've tried to talk to her about it, but she won't take a hint."

For a year and a half, Connie's mother was the focus of Connie's life. She was needed. She was Connie's best friend. And then she was dumped. No wonder she can't take a hint.

If you're in a situation like this, be extra gentle in disentangling yourself. You helped make this mess.

5

The Manipulators

MANIPULATORS ARE MASTERS of psychological warfare. They want you to do things their way, and no trick is too underhanded if it works. Their favorite weapon is guilt—which is scary, because guilt, as we all know, is the most powerful force in the universe.

On the surface, Manipulators may be any breed of parent—Advisers, Weaklings, Pushers—but strip off that thin veneer and you'll find a formidable opponent, one who can bring you to your knees, begging for mercy, with simple phrases like "This is going to kill your mother" or "After I've worked my fingers to the bone for you, how can you treat me like this?"

Who's in Control Here?

Manipulators control the relationship you have with them. They control when you visit, how long you stay, when you call them, how you talk to them, what you tell them, and how you treat them.

If there's any doubt in your mind about that, answer the following questions:

- Do you call your parents when *you* want to talk to them or when *they* want you to call?

- Are you selective about what you tell them for fear they'll disapprove of what you're doing?

- Do you smile and give in when you really feel like telling them where to go?

A yes to any of those questions means they are in control.

"But it's easier to give in," you say. "If I do it their way, I don't have to listen to my father yell, or watch my mother pout, or have them hang up on me, or hear them insinuate that I don't have time to bother with them."

Sure, it's easier. Don't you think your parents know that? They not only know it, they depend on it. They've spent years conditioning you that it's easier, that making them happy should be your number-one priority. All your life you've heard things like:

- "Be a good little girl (or boy), and stay quiet while Daddy takes a nap."

- "If you really loved me, you'd stop talking back all the time."

- "I can't tell you how happy we are that you're giving up those foolish notions of being a musician."

Your parents conditioned you in the finest Pavlovian tradition. They said: "Do things our way, and we will be happy. Make us happy, and you will get rewards. You will get ice cream and movies and the use of the car." The happier they were, the smoother things went.

If you were foolish enough to cross them and make them *un*happy, they pulled out the big guns—crying, screaming, sarcasm, blackmail, guilt, or whatever it took to change your mind—and squelched the rebellion.

Now, years later, the big guns are still being pulled out. And they still work.

But most of you don't see that. You don't want to admit that your parents long ago seized control of this relationship and that you've never gotten it back. You don't realize that while you're gritting your teeth, your parents are smiling with satisfaction. Because they've gotten their way. Again.

HOW TO COPE WITH MANIPULATORS

Manipulators are subtle, they're devious, and they've had years to perfect their technique. And their greatest achievement is that you have no idea what they're doing to you.

There is only one defense: Cut through the mirages and the misdirection and see them for what they really are. Realize that your parents are manipulating you to suit their own purposes.

Just as a magician's trick loses its impact once you know how it's done, guilt loses its power once you see that it's being used *intentionally* as a weapon.

From now on, when your parents try to manipulate you, shrug it off. Call them on it. Kid them about it. But don't give in to it.

Manipulators come in seven insidious varieties: the Saint, the Buck-Passer, the Martyr, the Hinter, the Scorekeeper, the Emotionally Distraught, and the Permanently Terminal.

THE SAINT

"I Would Never Have Treated My *Parents This Way."*

Saints are always right. They don't make mistakes, and they never have bad intentions. The daughter of one Saint said:

"My father told me over and over again what a good woman my mother was. My mother's friends told me repeatedly what a fine person my mother was. Even my mother told me how great she was. Naturally, such a good, fine, great woman as my mother couldn't be the cause of any unpleasantness, so when she and I had problems, I always assumed (and so did everybody else) that *I* was at fault. Throughout my childhood, it was my mother, the marvelous human being, versus me, her rotten kid. I didn't have a chance."

Because of numbness and tingling sensations in her right leg, Celeste's mother was admitted to the hospital for tests. She didn't tell Celeste she was going in, nor did she call her while she was there. She waited until she was being released, then called Celeste and said: "I hate to bother you, but I need a ride home. My friend Mabel brought me down here, but she's gone to visit her daughter in St. Paul. Could you pick me up?"

"Sure, Mom, where are you?"

"I'm at Eisenhower Memorial Hospital. But you'll have to stop at the front desk. The doctor won't release me until he knows someone's here to drive me home."

Of course, Celeste's mother got hours worth of the frantic, hysterical, "Why didn't you tell me?" reaction she was hoping for.

The message Saints deliver is "I'm a better person than you are," and they challenge you to match their Sainthood by being as good to *them* as they insist they were to you. You can't help but feel inadequate compared with such virtuous, self-denying, benevolent, and devoted human beings. How can you possibly return all their overwhelming generosity? How can you begin to live up to their high ideals and moral standards?

Saints even stockpile guilt for future use.

You're in a bind. You can't criticize Saints. You can't yell at them, question any of their decisions, or refuse any of their requests. And your parents know this. It's the perfect device for keeping you in line. If there's a conflict, they get to be always right, and you get to be always wrong.

"You Could Make Me So Happy, if Only You'd Try"

Many of you have swallowed this propaganda whole. You believe that problems or disagreements *are* your fault. You say, "My parents are nice old people who mean well, and if I were a better person, we'd get along fine." You blame yourself and your inadequacies as a son or daughter: "I feel terrible that I don't call my parents more than once a month." "I'm letting my parents down because I haven't gotten married yet." "I'm a schmuck because I dread my parents coming to visit."

It's amazing how often adult children let their gray-haired old parents off the hook by saying, "They mean well," "They're just looking out for my best interests," or "They're old; they can't help themselves."

Why all the excuses for your parents' behavior? How did you come to the conclusion that your parents are such noble creatures that they shouldn't be blamed for anything?

You didn't come up with that brilliant conclusion. Your parents did. They convinced you that, no matter what they did, their intentions were above reproach, that everything they did was for you, that they thought only of you. They hammered this into your conscious and subconscious by saying:

- "We never thought of ourselves."
- "Everything we did, we did for you."
- "We're doing this for your own good."
- "This hurts us more than it hurts you."
- "Nobody loves you like we do."

When you say, "My parents do the best they can," it's your parents talking, not you.

Let's face it. You've been brainwashed.

I Remember Mama

Saints are particularly noble about how well they treated *their* parents. Your father says with disdain, "We never let a month go by without visiting my parents. But we're lucky if you show up twice a year." Your mother says, "I wrote to my parents every week from the day I left home until the day they died. Why can't you do the same for us?"

Since time has a way of playing tricks on your parents' memories, jolt them back to reality by asking as innocently as you can, "Were you happy doing that? Wasn't it sometimes inconvenient?" And the clincher: "So you want me to feel the same way about you that you did about your parents?"

The Infallible Parents

Even when your parents are obviously manipulating you, they have so thoroughly convinced you that they're acting in your best interests, that you defend them. *You* take the blame: Maybe it *was* your fault things didn't work out.

Your mother may say worriedly, "I don't know, maybe we were wrong. Maybe we should have let you go to that out-of-state college that you wanted to go to so badly." Even though she knows she didn't let you go out of state because she couldn't stand the thought of your being so far away. But she doesn't want to admit it. She wants you to respond with "That's okay, Mom. Going to Hometown U. really worked out best for me in the long run." She wants you to confirm that she was indeed a good selfless mother.

And you will. You won't tell her the truth. You won't tell her: "Going to Hometown U. was the worst thing that ever happened to me. It's the reason I've been so unhappy for the last ten years. I hated that school; it didn't give degrees that any prospective employer would respect. Furthermore, that's where I had the disastrous love affair with Terry, which warped me for life on relationships. How could you have done that to me?"

If you said that, your mother would have a stroke. So you let your parents off the hook. You buy into their version of reality, and you blame yourself: "They meant well, and if I had tried harder, I probably could have made my years at Hometown U. work out."

Why not say instead, "They're wrong, totally and completely wrong." Or "Who are they kidding? They're doing this for themselves, not for me." Or "My parents don't have the faintest idea how to handle certain things."

And why don't you start saying it to them?

THE BUCK-PASSER

"It Doesn't Matter to Me, Of Course, but It Will Kill Your Father [or Mother]."

Buck-Passers don't hold *themselves* up as Saints; instead they canonize your *other* parent. When they don't like what you're doing, they point at your other parent (or sometimes your spouse, your children, your grandparents, or one of your close personal friends) and say, "I can take it, but they can't." Examples include "Your father will be so upset" or "Your mother will never get over this."

They call upon you to make a sacrifice, to give up what you're doing to please this marvelous, self-sacrificing, sensitive other parent—because they don't have the nerve to tell you how *they* feel.

Buck-Passers often try to cover up what they're doing by saying, "Don't mention this to your father [or whoever the

Buck-*Receiver* is]. He wouldn't like it if he knew I'd said anything to you."

Don't buy it. Run, don't walk, to your other parent and spill the beans—preferably in the presence of the Buck-Passer. Then get both of them to fess up to who really thinks what.

THE MARTYR

"Don't Worry About Us. . . . Somehow We'll Survive the Tragedy of Your Not Coming over for Dinner on Sunday."

Cindy, a thirty-two-year-old customer service representative, said:

> "I only have two weeks of vacation, and every year it leads to a big conflict with my parents. I want to go *on vacation,* like to Miami or Acapulco, but my parents want me to come 'home' and spend it with them. The problem is that they never tell me that's what they want.
>
> "Every year when I try to break the news to them that I'm not coming home, my mother says, 'Honey, don't you worry about us for a minute. I know it's been months since we've seen you, but you deserve a nice, relaxing time with your friends at a resort somewhere. Good heavens, I can understand why you wouldn't want to spend your vacation with a couple of old fuddy-duddies like your father and me. We're disappointed, of course, but we'll be all right.'
>
> "I feel so guilty that I always end up in Nebraska with them, instead of on a cruise with my friends."

Translating Messages from Martyrs

Martyrs deliver two different messages: the one they say and the one they mean. Your ears hear "I'd love to try that new Chinese restaurant," but your brain registers "I hate Chinese food, which you know, so why are you suggesting that place?"

All it takes is a slight inflection of the voice, an excessive dose of pleasantness, or a vaguely phony smile, and suddenly you get the feeling you've screwed up.

The double message is often hard to recognize, so to get you started, here's a translation of what Cindy's mother said:

MOM SAID	MOM MEANT
Honey, don't you worry about us for a minute.	Don't worry about your vacation; worry about the fact that you're hurting our feelings.
It's been months since we've seen you,	Check your calendar. It's been four months, twelve days, six hours, and twenty-three minutes since we last saw you. We sit here month after month without seeing you, with hardly a phone call and never a letter, but what do you care?
but you deserve a nice, relaxing time	Sure, you're the only one who works hard. We don't do a thing. What about what *we* deserve?
with your friends	You are so immature and shallow that your friends mean more to you than your parents do.
at a resort somewhere.	Isn't it nice that some people can afford to go to an expensive hotel? On our income, we're lucky if we can go to Red Lobster once a month for dinner.
Good heavens, I can understand why you wouldn't want to spend your vacation with a couple of old fuddy-duddies like your father and me.	You'll be sorry if these two old fuddy-duddies drop dead while you're lying on a beach somewhere.

We're disappointed, of course,	Disappointed? We're devastated.
but we'll be all right.	We'll kill ourselves.

The only way to deal with Martyrs is to ignore the underlying message and take them at their word. If your parents can't be adult enough or honest enough to tell you what they really want, they don't deserve to get it.

When your parents say, "Don't worry about us," respond with "Oh, good, I knew you'd understand. Thanks for being such great parents."

If they complain later, say with bright-eyed innocence, "But you said not to worry. I thought you meant it."

Martyrs use guilt because it works. Tune it out.

THE HINTER

"This May Be off the Subject, but Have You Ever Thought About . . . ?"

Hinters are a little more direct than Martyrs. They make subtle suggestions; they make remarks in passing; they imply. They never make direct statements that might get them accused of meddling.

For example:

- A father who doesn't like your fiancé, but doesn't want to say so, says, "Have you set a wedding date yet? No? I think you're smart not to rush into anything. You've got *years* to get married."

- In the middle of a conversation about work, a mother slips in a hint about visiting: "I'm sorry to hear you're so overloaded at work. With all that on your mind, don't even *think* about visiting us. Just come whenever you can."

- A mother who's concerned that you might move in with someone you're not legally, officially, and thoroughly married to says, "In my day, that just wasn't done. I realize, of course, that times have changed."

Hinters rely on the fact that you won't confront them. But confronting them is the only way to get them to stop.

When Dad says he's glad you're taking your time getting married, call him on it.

> **YOU:** Don't you want me to get married?
>
> **DAD:** I didn't say that. I was just agreeing with your decision to wait.
>
> **YOU:** I know, but it sounded as if you *want* me to wait. Do you have a problem with my getting married?

When Mom sneaks in the mention of a visit, don't let it go by.

> **YOU:** Is that a hint, Mom?
>
> **MOM** (INNOCENTLY): No, of course not. I just meant...you know...not to worry about us.
>
> **YOU** (PUZZLED): But we weren't talking about my visiting you —or my worrying about you for that matter. We were talking about work.

Let them know that they're not as subtle as they think. It takes all the fun out of it.

THE SCOREKEEPER
"You Should See What Your Sister Bought Me!"

What Scorekeepers, like all Manipulators, want is more— more attention, more affection, more gifts, or more cooperation—and to get it, they try to draw you into a bidding war with your brothers or sisters. They recount, with great relish, the many delightful and often expensive things your brothers or sisters have done for them—and point out, directly or indirectly, that your efforts pale by comparison.

"For your father's and my anniversary," Yvonne's mother reported excitedly, "your brother took us out to the most fabulous restaurant. He hired a limousine to pick us up and bought me a corsage—it was just marvelous.

"By the way, dear," her voice drops, "thank you for the nice card. It was so sweet of you to remember us."

You could hear Yvonne's teeth grinding for almost three blocks.

Some Scorekeepers are more direct: "Your sister calls us every day. How come we hear from you only once a month?"

This is manipulation at its finest. The Scorekeepers' message is that you don't love them as much if you don't spend as much time, effort, or money on them as your angelic brothers or sisters do.

Don't let it bother you. Instead of reaching for your wallet to relieve all this guilt, jump into the back-patting fray with them. Say sincerely, "Freddy's a helluva guy, isn't he? He must have spent a fortune!"

If Freddy wants to go broke fawning all over your parents, that's his business. *But don't feel like you have to, too.* Your parents, like well-mannered people everywhere, should be encouraging you to spend *less* money on them, not more.

As for attention and affection, tell them, "I don't have time to call you every day, but that doesn't mean I'm not thinking about you," or "You know I'm not very demonstrative, but that doesn't mean I don't love you."

Give them a small dose of the reassurance they're looking for, and leave it at that. If you try to up the ante on your extravagant siblings, you'll find yourself in a game you can't win.

THE EMOTIONALLY DISTRAUGHT
"Now You've Really Upset Me!"

When you do something the Emotionally Distraught don't like, they cry, sulk, pout, beg, plead, get sarcastic, yell, scream, slam doors, refuse to speak to you, or storm out. They do everything but sit down like a couple of adults and have a rational discussion about the problem.

If you say, "I won't be home for Christmas," they don't ask with polite concern, "Oh? Is there a problem?"

They scream, "How can you do this to us! You *know* this is our favorite holiday. It will be ruined if you're not here. Why, we might as well not have Christmas at all."

They make you feel so guilty that you find yourself blathering, "Did I say I *wasn't* coming home for Christmas? No, no, no. I meant I *was* coming home for Christmas. You misunderstood me. I'll not only be home for Christmas, I'll be there for New Year's Eve, Martin Luther King's Birthday, the Super Bowl, Valentine's Day, Washington's Birthday, St. Patrick's Day, Easter, Secretaries Day..."

Steel yourself. Remember that the Emotionally Distraught's tirades are carefully calculated to make you do it their way. It's a performance they reserve exclusively for their children. They don't do this to their friends; they do it only to you. They may be genuinely upset, but they are also genuinely and completely determined to change your mind.

Don't go toe-to-toe with them. They can raise the emotional pitch way beyond your ability to handle it. So just walk away. Say, "I'm sorry you're so upset. I'll call you later when you've had a chance to calm down, and we'll talk about it then." Then leave. (Make sure, if you have bad news to deliver, that you do it at a time and place that you can escape from without making a scene.)

That's not callous; that's simply refusing to play their game.

THE PERMANENTLY TERMINAL
"We're Not Going to Be Around Much Longer, and After We're Gone ..."

The death of your parents is such a frightening possibility that most of us can't bear to think about it. But the Permanently Terminals *want* you to think about it, because it has the potential for the granddaddy of all guilt trips: Your parents die, and you realize you didn't make them happy in their last few precious years. Or, worse, you upset them so badly that they drop over dead. You'd never forgive yourself.

The Permanently Terminal's message is twofold:

1. "Be nice to me, because I'm old and I might die any day now."

2. "If you're mean to me, I might die right this minute."

Excuse me if this sounds morbid, but death is inevitable. Sooner or later (hopefully, later) your parents are going to die. Chances are, though, that since they've lived this long, they aren't going to die tomorrow.

But if they do, it won't be your fault (unless, out of sheer exasperation, you throw them in front of a train). Despite what your parents want you to believe, you don't have the power to kill them by not coming over for dinner on Sunday. You can't give them a cerebral hemorrhage or a cardiac arrest by saying, "I don't have time to talk to you right now." And you won't cause them to expire if you tell them to stop calling you at seven o'clock on Saturday mornings.

If they do get mad and die, their death was purely coincidental. If they get mad because you want to have a normal, adult relationship with them, *they made themselves mad by being unreasonable,* and their death was still purely coincidental.

Remember that the constant references to their advanced age and frail health are their way of controlling you. They *want* you to be afraid.

One woman said:

"My mother insists that every visit end with both of us saying, 'I love you.' That way, if one of us dies before the next time we see each other, our last words will have been a statement of affection.

"This really annoys me, because I see her several times a week. But I'm afraid not to do it—what if she did die?"

How to Handle the Nearly Dead

We're not talking here about parents who are seriously ill or who have major medical problems; they deserve special consideration. We're talking about the fakers and hypochondriacs.

Your best defense with these phonies is to be deadly serious (if you'll pardon the pun) about their symptoms.

When your mother says, "I feel faint," don't lead her to the couch, put an ice pack on her head, and beg her to get medical attention—all the while apologizing for having upset her so much. That's exactly what she's looking for.

Call her bluff by calling her doctor. If it's after office hours, call his answering service and have him paged. If your mother doesn't have a regular doctor, call the nearest hospital emergency room and ask if you should bring her in.

The Permanently Terminal want attention, not medical bills, and this game is no fun if it's going to cost them a fortune to play it.

Be Philosophical About It

With parents who don't have symptoms, but just like to remind you that their days are numbered, don't give them the emotional reaction they're looking for. If you show fear, they'll know they've got you.

Cry your eyes out at home alone about their impending demise, if you must, but to their face say only, "You've been around this long—I'm sure you're going to be around a lot longer." Then change the subject.

6

The Moaners-and-Groaners, the Mean-and-Nasties, and the Bullies

NEGATIVE PARENTS don't subscribe to the philosophy of "If you can't say something good, don't say anything at all." If they did, they'd have to take a vow of silence. No, their motto is "Life's a bitch, and then you die."

No positive ray of sunshine permeates these parents' gloomy existence, because nobody—including you, God, and the federal government—does anything right. And these parents can't wait to tell you all about it.

Being around the Moaners-and-Groaners, the Mean-and-Nasties, and the Bullies is depressing. Their black-hole view of the universe is demoralizing, their personal attacks are intimidating, and their lack of cheerfulness is draining.

Back in the bad old days when you were a child, there was no escape from these disaster-mongers. You had to listen to their tirades, put up with their disgusted sighing, and endure their perpetual bad moods.

But fortunately the bad old days are over. You may not have realized it, but you don't have to put up with negative parents ever again. Today, you can escape.

HOW TO COPE WITH NEGATIVE PARENTS

The rules for dealing with negative parents are simple:

1. Ask them to lighten up. If they don't lighten up, leave.
2. Don't let them intimidate, depress, or upset you. Realize that their problems are not your problems.
3. Don't waste your time trying to change negative parents into positive parents. It's too late for that.

Easier said than done, of course, but here's how to use those three simple rules with the seven types of negative parents: the Complainer, the Morose, the Detractor, the Insulter, the Insult Collector, the Tyrant, and the Bully.

THE COMPLAINER

"Have You Seen the Prices of Gasoline, Toothpaste, Doughnuts, and the Movies Lately?"

Everybody complains now and then, but Complainers have the market cornered. For them, every cloud has an even blacker lining, and only three things are certain in this world: death, taxes, and the fact that there will never be a solution to their problems.

Rhonda called her mother one day and invited her out to lunch.

"I can't go," her mother said. "I don't have anything to wear."

"You always say you don't have anything to wear," Rhonda said. "Why don't you go out and buy some clothes?"

"Because everything is so expensive."

"This is January, Mom. All the winter clothes are on sale."

"I'm not going to buy anything until I lose fifteen pounds.

There's no point in buying clothes now that will have to be altered later."

Rhonda silently counted to ten and asked, "Mom, how long have you been talking about losing fifteen pounds?"

"I don't know. A while, I guess."

"Try four years."

"Well, the only place I go is out to lunch with you once a month. That's hardly worth buying new clothes for," her mother said.

"Lunch with me doesn't have to be the only time you leave the house, you know. The people at the library want you to work there three days a week. Why don't you do that?"

"I can't do that," her mother said. "I don't have anything to wear."

For Complainers, every situation is hopeless, and change, in any direction, just makes it worse.

During the high-interest, high-inflation days of the late seventies, one retired father blew a gasket every time someone hit the "total" key on a cash register. "With prices going up like this, I'll never be able to live on my pension," he griped.

Seven years later, during the low-interest, low-inflation days of the mid-eighties, he was still mad. "With interest rates going down like this," he grumbled, "I'll never be able to live off my savings."

Some Complainers bellyache even when there isn't a problem.

Martin took his parents out to dinner as a present for their thirty-fifth anniversary. As soon as they were seated, Martin's dad started complaining. "I get mad every time I come here," he said, "because I know they're going to overcharge me."

Not believing his ears, Martin said, "Unless you've decided to buy your own anniversary dinner, Dad, there's nothing to be mad about. I hate to disappoint you, but tonight they're going to overcharge *me*."

A Directory of Complainers

Complainers vary somewhat in how they respond to the sad fact that nothing is right with the world.

Grouches are infuriated by everything. Everything is a personal insult, including stray dogs, the way other people drive, and the weather—to name a few.

Pessimists are convinced that not only are things bad but they're going to get worse. They're looking for world-record problems ("You think it's hot now? The weather service is predicting that this will be the worst heat wave of the century."), and they're disappointed when they don't get them.

Nostalgics remember back when everything was better. Prices were lower, products were of higher quality, and people were nicer. "We never had to lock our doors at night when I was growing up," they say with remorse. "I don't know what's happened to the world."

Defeatists refuse to waste their time on foolishness like hope. There is no solution, it's never going to be better, and you just have to learn to live life in the toilet. Their favorite expression is "What did you expect?"

What, Me Solve It?

It is a natural response, when people dump their problems all over you, to do one of two things: (1) give them advice or (2) try to solve the problem for them. When those people are your parents, you feel doubly responsible. They're having trouble, they're old, they're unhappy, and you should fix it.

But Complainers don't want advice, and they don't want solutions. What they want from you is sympathy. They want you to confirm their view of the world by saying, "Yeah, I agree, life stinks." (If you also believe life stinks, you and your parents probably get along just fine—at least on this point—so you can skip the next few pages.)

Complainers *like* to complain. They've been doing it for years. It's not a very pleasant way of life, but it's *their* way of life, and you'll never get them to give it up. All you can do is get them to stop complaining *at you.*

How to Get Out of the Complaint Department

For some parents, complaining is a habit, and they go on and on without realizing how much griping they're doing. So your first line of attack should be indirect and noncon-frontational.

Point out how much complaining they're doing. Ask them lightly, "Don't you get tired of complaining about everything?" (If you remember the Introduction to this book, that question worked quite well with my father.)

Try a little humor. Laugh and say, "Gee, I'm getting totally depressed here. Can we change the subject, or should I just go jump off a tall building?"

Escalate their complaints, hoping they'll take a hint. Say, "You're right, Dad, about all the crime in New York City, and it's probably just a matter of time before that crime wave hits here in Clarksburg. Old Mr. Mitchell across the street looks pretty dangerous to me. Aren't you afraid he might come over here, knock you out with his walker, and take everything you own?"

Do this sort of chiding with good humor, and you'll get away with it.

The next time they start complaining, continue teasing them: "Uh-oh, Dad's on a tear again. We'd better notify the police in case he decides to get out his twelve-gauge and go shoot the mayor."

If you can get a Complainer to laugh, you've got the battle half won.

The Direct Method

When the more subtle method fails, try bringing Complainers back to reality with these two questions:

"Is there anything you can do about it?" Force this to a yes or no answer. If it's yes, suggest diplomatically that they put up or shut up. If they can do something about the problem, why don't they?

If they can't, tell them: "I understand that it bothers you, but you admit you can't do anything about it. So either make the best of it or forget about it."

Some Complainers sidestep this question by saying, "I suppose there's something I could do about it, but it's not worth it. It probably wouldn't change anything." In which case you should answer, "If you're not willing to try to fix it, why do you keep complaining about it?"

"What do you think should be done about it?" Obviously your parents can't do anything about global issues like crime or the national debt—that's why those topics are so much fun to complain about. But by asking what *should* be done, you can at least shift them from a problem orientation to a solution orientation. You never know, it may lead to a lively discussion of public hangings as a solution for crime—or even as a cure for the national debt.

Bow Out

If neither the subtle nor the direct method shuts off the Complainer, exit stage left. Say, "This is getting too heavy for me. I think I'll go out for a milkshake. Anybody care to join me?"

Then go.

When You Are the Source of Complaints

Some Complainers not only think the world is a drag, they think *you* are a drag. Their line is *"You* and what *you're* doing make me miserable."

Tell them to quit. Tell them to cease and desist, or you'll stop coming around to ruin their day.

> **THE COMPLAINER:** You never come to see me anymore.
> **YOU:** That's because when I get here, all you ever do is complain that I never come to see you anymore. I'm tired of listening to you complain about me. Stop it. Now.

Parents who insist that you are the cause of their misery are rude and irresponsible. You may not be perfect, but *they* control whether or not that bothers them. If you're a bum, they have the right to tell you to leave them alone. They *don't* have the right to whine at you ad infinitum.

If you're not a bum, then they really have no right to give you a hard time. And they deserve to be told, in no uncertain terms, to back off.

THE MOROSE

" 'How's Everything?' I'll Tell You How Everything Is—It's Terrible."

Abe Lincoln said that most people are just about as happy as they make up their minds to be, and Morose parents have made up their minds to be miserable. Everything makes them unhappy.

> Sam's mother was in a permanently bad mood. She was pleased when Sam came to visit, but it didn't last. She couldn't enjoy dinner because the roast didn't come out exactly right,

she was having trouble with one of her friends, the dry cleaners had ruined her favorite sweater, and she wasn't sleeping well.

Every visit was a strain for Sam as he tried new and different ways to cheer up his mother. For every complaint, he tried to find a solution. He planned activities that might take her mind off her problems. But nothing ever worked, and by the time he left, Sam was as depressed as his mother was.

Nothing worked for Sam, because nothing *can* work. Sam's mother has decided to be unhappy; she probably decided it years ago. And no matter what Sam does, he won't be able to change her mind.

It is not your responsibility, nor is it even in your power, to make your parents happy. If they choose to be sad or grouchy or anxious all the time, that's their *choice*. You can't change it. You have to allow them to feel the way they want to feel.

But if it will ease your conscience, have a heart-to-heart talk with them about it:

"You are unhappy all the time. And by being unhappy, you upset the rest of us. Does it bother you to be this way? Do you want help? The only thing we won't do for you is participate in feeling bad. If you want to do that, you'll have to do it by yourself."

Don't expect long-term results. The Morose will apologize for putting a damper on everything, will be cheerful for a short while, then will go right back to being dejected.

Many of these parents need professional care (they are clinically depressed), but few are willing to get it.

Maureen pointed out to her father that being unhappy had become routine behavior for him. "Why don't you see somebody?" she said as gently as possible. "You're depressed, and depression is treatable."

Her father laughed. "You'd have to be crazy to see a psychiatrist," he said, not recognizing the sad humor in his comment. "They're all a bunch of quacks."

If your parents won't get help, stop making it your problem.

If you can accept that your parents' happiness is not your responsibility, the Morose become more tolerable. They are an object of pity, perhaps, but they are no longer your burden. You can say, "Gee, I'm sorry you're unhappy," and leave it at that.

THE DETRACTOR

"I Know You're Happy Now, but Consider All the Things that Could Go Wrong."

Detractors are not only miserable, but they want *you* to be miserable, too. They can take the shine off any situation.

YOU: Great news—I've been offered a job with the Global Computer Company.

THE DETRACTOR: Haven't you heard? The computer industry is in a slump. You'll probably be laid off before you can get your name put on the door.

YOU: I had the most terrific dinner at the Plaza Club last night.

THE DETRACTOR: It's not a bad place, if you don't mind paying totally outrageous prices for food.

YOU: I'm going to be in the lottery drawing. The jackpot is up to $5.6 million!

THE DETRACTOR: You won't win, and even if you do, the Internal Revenue Service will take most of it.

And, as is the case with so many other types of parents, there's no use arguing with Detractors.

YOU: I know the computer industry has had some trouble, but Global Computer's sales have been going up steadily.

THE DETRACTOR: Until now, that is.

YOU: But they've got a brand-new product that will revolutionize the market.

THE DETRACTOR: That's what Ford said about the Edsel.

YOU: But this is a promotion for me. I'll be the head of the human resources department.

THE DETRACTOR: They're always the first to go when a company has to lay people off. Besides, nobody ever became president of a company by working in the personnel department. It's a dead-end job.

The Life of the Party

Detractors are a big hit at funerals, house fires, and major car accidents, but other than that, they're about as entertaining as Limburger cheese. Nothing is ever good enough to earn their unqualified praise or enthusiasm. Your 10 percent raise should have been a 15 percent raise. Your new house should have been in a nicer neighborhood. Your newborn daughter should have been a son.

Isn't it sad? Detractors have such an aversion to seeing other people happy that they can't stand seeing their own kids enjoying themselves. They claim to be realists, but they're really just spoilsports.

Let them know you realize what's going on: that they want company in their misery. But tell them they've got the wrong person for the wrong job:

"You really can't stand to see me happy, can you? What you call realism, I call pessimism. So you know what? I think I'll go find an optimist to share my good mood, my good news, or my good fortune with."

THE INSULTER

"If You Had Half a Brain in Your Head, Which You Don't..."

Somebody please explain this to me: Why do some of you get worse treatment from your parents (not to mention other family members) than you do from a perfect stranger who doesn't know you from a sledload of spit?

I don't get it.

Your parents are supposed to love you, aren't they? Then why does your father say things to you that would get his nose broken for him at work? Why does your mother make remarks that would cause open warfare at her bridge club?

Insulters throw the rules of etiquette out the window when dealing with their own children.

> A sudden cold snap found Christie without a winter coat during a March visit to her parents in Illinois. Her mother said, "You can wear my coat; there's nowhere I need to go today"—even though she was four inches shorter and two dress sizes smaller than the somewhat hefty Christie.
>
> "Mom," Christie laughed, "there's no way I could fit into your coat."
>
> Her father threw a disgusted look her way and said, "Maybe you could if you'd lose twenty pounds."

"I'm Better than You Are"

Your parents use insults to make themselves feel superior to you. They want to bring you down, not only to their level but below. One father said about his son: "I raised this kid, and I taught him everything he knows. What could *he* possibly tell *me* about anything?"

Of course, the age-difference insult works no matter

how old you are. It ranges from "You're only fourteen—what do you know?" to "You're only forty-seven; you have no idea of the problems I have at my age."

Try Not to Kill Them

Remember the psychologists who said your parents had the power to turn you into either the next Mother Teresa or the next Hillside Strangler? Well, they're no help here, either. They recommend that you try to visualize Insulters as small children who didn't get enough love from their own parents and realize that they're just lashing out for the mistreatment they experienced years ago. That's supposed to make the insulting parent seem less intimidating and offensive.

I'm not a psychologist, but my untrained, nonprofessional opinion is that if your father or mother insults you, you should, as gracefully as possible, tell that particular parent to go take a flying leap.

I'm serious. You don't have to put up with insults from anybody, particularly not from your parents.

On the outside chance that your parents can take a hint, start with "I'm sure you didn't mean that. I'll come back later when you're in a better mood."

Then leave. Get up and walk out. Don't wait for a reply; just go. If they try to stop you with "Don't walk out on me when I'm talking to you," stop dead in your tracks, and ask with as little malice and as much curiosity as you can muster: "Why would I stay here and let you insult me?"

Then stand there and wait for a response. Don't run off. Act as if you honestly want their opinion (which maybe you do).

Whatever you do, don't let this degenerate into a shouting match. Yelling moves the relationship backward, not forward. If you want your parents to treat *you* with respect, treat *them* with respect—no matter how badly they act.

But if it gets dicey, get out.

Is There Anything Funny About This?

There's not much funny about parents who are insulting, but if you can possibly find something to laugh about, it helps take the sting out. One son said:

> "When my father thinks you've said something stupid, he'll fix you with one of his 'You must be joking' stares, push his glasses up on his nose, and mutter 'I suppose that's so,' as if he's humoring the village idiot. Then he'll wander off or start reading the newspaper as if you're not there anymore.
>
> "It used to make me want to choke him.
>
> "Then one day I said something to my wife that, well, *could* have been construed as stupid, and she looked at me, pushed her glasses up on her nose, and sighed, 'I suppose that's so.' It was such a perfect imitation of my father that I broke up laughing. It's become a joke between us, and now when my father does it, it's funny instead of aggravating."

They Are Supposed to Love You, But...

Not all parents like their children.

Oh, they love you—they have to, because you're their child—but they may not be crazy about you as a person. A very macho father may not like his bookish son. A Betty Crocker-type mother may be uncomfortable with her aggressive businesswoman daughter. One or both parents may feel that your birth trapped them in a life they didn't want.

You may remind them of a brother or an aunt they dislike. They may not approve of the friends you have, your attitude toward work, or the way you live.

And that disappointment and disapproval may surface as rude, unkind behavior.

If that's the case, you have only one choice: Cut your visits with them down to the lowest tolerable (for you) level, and spend your time instead with people who do like you.

Don't torture yourself trying to get affection from people who don't have it to give.

THE INSULT COLLECTOR

"I Know I Didn't Tell You I Was in the Hospital, but That Was No Reason Not to Visit Me."

Insult Collectors are just the opposite of Insulters. They try to get *you* to insult *them.*

They use birthdays, anniversaries, national and religious holidays, invitations, the U.S. Mail, and anything else they can get their hands on, to make you feel guilty about how poorly you treat them.

To show you how this works, let's say you have a bad memory for dates. You ought to remember birthdays and anniversaries, but you don't—and that's an Insult Collector's dream. They wouldn't think of helping you out. They don't remind you. They don't call and say, "Father's Day is the day after tomorrow," or "Your mother's birthday is next week."

No, they don't say a word. They stare at the calendar for a month, watching the days go by, waiting for you—their coldhearted, unfeeling offspring—to let your mother's birthday pass unnoticed, unmarked, and uncelebrated (at least by you), thereby breaking her heart and ruining any chance of happiness for her for the next twelve months.

And, of course, bright and early on the day after your mother's birthday, your phone rings and you hear your father say, "You couldn't have called your mother on her birthday? This saint of a woman who changed your diapers and saved pin money to send you to college, who worked her fingers to the bone for you all those years? You couldn't remember your *mother's* birthday? What? No, you can't talk to her. She's too upset."

It's Groveling Time

The goal of all Insult Collectors is to force you to grovel for their forgiveness.

If you commit an atrocity like forgetting Mother's Day, you're doomed to hours of begging her forgiveness and to spending most of next month's paycheck trying to make it up to her.

The advantage for your mother is that she gets ten times more affection, compliments, gifts, candy, and flowers than she would have if you had remembered Mother's Day in the first place.

And she feels noble and superior, and gets to be a martyr with all her friends. ("You think you've got problems? *My* daughter forgot *Mother's Day.*")

Innovative Insult Collecting

In between birthdays, anniversaries, and major holidays, Insult Collectors have to settle for what they can get.

Visits. Insult Collectors like to invite you over: "Why don't you drop by on Saturday. Any time will be fine."

"I will if I get a chance," you say hesitantly, "but Jimmy's got baseball practice, and Susie has her piano lesson. I don't think I'll have time, but I'll try."

Most people realize that "I'll try" means "Probably not." But not Insult Collectors. They call you on Sunday afternoon and say, "You said you'd be here at three o'clock yesterday. What happened?"

And watch out if *you* bring up the visit. "We might drive over next weekend." *Might* to the rest of the world means *maybe*—maybe we'll be there, maybe we won't. To Insult Collectors, it means you promised. If you cancel out, you've ruined their plans. They were counting on it; they stocked up on all the kids' favorite foods. Why, it never occurred to them that you might *not* come.

Remarks—casual or otherwise. Insult Collectors can make an insult out of anything—including the way you say good morning.

> **YOU:** Hey, Dad, I forgot to ask how your check up went. Is everything okay?
>
> **DAD:** I wondered when you'd get around to asking—my check up was two weeks ago. It's heartwarming to know you're so concerned about my health.

> **YOU:** Mom, it looks as if you're having a little trouble getting the geraniums going this year.
>
> **MOM:** I can't do everything around here, you know. It's not enough that I spend all day cooking and cleaning so the house will be nice when you show up and you'll have something to eat? I've got to have flowers, too?

Assignments. Consciously or unconsciously, Insult Collectors look for ways to set you up. They give you assignments without asking if you want the job, and are mad when you don't fulfill the responsibility they gave you.

Your mother sends you photographs and newspaper clippings, and tells you to send them on to your brother when you're finished with them. The photos and clippings end up in a drawer somewhere, while your mother calls you weekly demanding to know why your brother hasn't received them. You never do send them, and you beg your mother not to send any more, but a month later another packet arrives in the mail with the same instructions: "Send these along to your brother when you're finished with them."

Dismantling an Insult Collector's Collection

Short-circuit the Insult Collector with these tactics:

Get help. You have no option but to remember birthdays, anniversaries, and holidays. No amount of pleading a bad memory or a busy schedule will get you off the hook.

So appoint somebody, anybody—your spouse, one of your kids, your next-door neighbor, or somebody at work —even if you have to pay them—to keep track of your parents' birthdays and anniversary and all those major holidays. Have this duly appointed representative buy a card, stick it under your nose, then make you sign it and address the envelope. Have this person put a stamp on the card and put it in a mailbox.

(*Caution:* Don't have the envelope addressed by somebody whose handwriting your parents won't recognize. They'll really be mad then: "You had to *hire* somebody to remind you that we're still alive?")

Have this same hired gun badger you until you arrange to see your parents on these hallowed occasions—or at least until you call them.

Make no vague promises. Avoid problems in areas other than holidays by never, ever mentioning to your parents that you *might* visit them next Thursday or drop in at their New Year's Eve party or take them to the movies. Not until you have absolutely decided beyond any shadow of a doubt, not until you have bought your plane tickets or gassed up the car and put the luggage in the trunk, should you let your parents in on your plans.

If they invite you to something, decline the invitation unless you are 100 percent certain that you will attend. Quickly and firmly, say no. Show no ambivalence. Remember, to Insult Collectors, a maybe is as good as a guarantee. If you waiver, you've had it.

Be alert for an ambush. Insult Collectors make casual comments that come back to haunt you later. On Monday they mention that their car needs work, and that they'll probably take it to the dealership on Friday. On Thursday night, they call and tell you to pick them up at 7:00 A.M.

"But I can't," you protest. "I've got a breakfast meeting at seven o'clock."

Indignant, the Insult Collector replies, "I told you I had to take the car in for servicing on Friday morning. I thought you realized I'd need someone to pick me up."

So ask at every opportunity, "Is that something you want me to help you with?" You can always say no, but you will have at least gotten the hidden agenda out on the table.

Of course, Insult Collectors will ignore any of *your* casual comments if it helps them get the drop on you. While menu planning for your next visit, your mother will conveniently "forget" that you mentioned you were on a diet. Then she'll be offended when you don't want to eat her special pasta with heavy cream sauce.

Use preventive measures. Head off problems as early as possible. Weeks before you're scheduled to arrive at your parents' house, start calling your mother to warn her that you're on a diet and won't be pigging out as usual during your visit. As for the Mad Mailer, tell her that if she wants you to send things on to your brother she'd better also send you a stamped envelope with his name and address on it—or else he won't get it. Better yet, insist that she send the stuff to your brother *first,* and make him mail it to you.

Don't let it bother you. Preventive measures are no guarantee that you still won't get chocolate cake or packages of clippings. Your parents may ignore your requests and make you sixteen kinds of dessert or keep right on trying to use you as a branch of the U.S. Postal Service. If they do, it's hostile, aggressive behavior that means "What *I* want is what's important; I don't care what you want."

All you need to say is, "Sorry, I tried to warn you. That you decided not to take me seriously is your problem, not mine."

There's no good way to completely stop Insult Collectors, because they are so amazingly inventive—and sensitive. For some twisted reason they like to feel bad, and they want you to feel responsible. But who needs people who want you to feel rotten?

Do your best, apologize if you hurt their feelings, then don't feel guilty about it for another minute.

THE TYRANT

"Don't You Dare Do That in This House!"

Tyrants (usually fathers) issue commands and bark orders. They tell you what to do, when to do it, and how to do it. They intimidate you with tone, volume, or both, but the message is the same: "Do it my way, or you'll be sorry."

You cross a Tyrant at your own risk. Of course, most of you wouldn't dream of crossing them. "When my father tells you how he wants things done," one son said, "you know you'd better hop to, or else."

But the question is: "or else" what? Or else Dad's going to spank you? Or throw a temper tantrum? Or send you to your room? What are you afraid he'll do?

Why Are You Still Afraid of Your Parents?

You're operating off old information. Very old information. When you were four feet tall and weighed fifty-five pounds, having a six-foot, two hundred-pound man mad at you was pretty scary. You were convinced, at the most primal level of your little being, that your life was on the line.

Sure, Daddy loved you, but what if he went berserk and killed you? As Bill Cosby said to his kids, "I brought you into this world, and I can take you back out again." And you knew that was true.

So it was better not to take any chances; better to straighten up and fly right, and try to make it to age twenty-one alive.

But that was then, and this is now, and your subconscious needs to get the message that, as an adult, you can say whatever you want to Mommy and Daddy—as long as you're reasonable about it—and you won't be physically maimed or emotionally discarded. Old Dad won't haul off and crack you in the mouth, and Mom won't pack her bags and disappear. It's time to give up that old fear that stops you from saying or doing anything that might upset your parents.

Stop for a minute and ask yourself what would really happen if you said, "Stop shouting." Or "There's no need to treat me as if I'm ten years old." Or "You don't know what you're talking about."

Would the world come to an end?

Unenlisting in Dad's Army

You're too old to be "straightened out" by dear old Dad, so tell him to knock it off. Tell him nicely, or tell him firmly, or even tell him nonverbally, like Jerry did:

> Jerry was helping his parents move to a new house. It was slow going, because his mother spent more time reminiscing than she did packing. When she got to the box of vacation souvenirs, she cornered Jerry for almost half an hour.
>
> Meanwhile, in the backyard, Jerry's dad was fuming, waiting for Jerry to help him load the lawn mower into the truck. Finally he yelled, "Jerry, get down here right now."
>
> Jerry's hackles went up. He went down to the garage, but instead of apologizing and scurrying around, he walked right up to his father, looked him square in the eye, and said in a quiet but stern voice, "What do you want, Dad, and why are you shouting?"
>
> Surprised at this challenge, Jerry's father was momentarily speechless. Then *he* started scrambling: "Well, I just want to get this lawn mower in the truck. Say, did I, uh, mention how much I appreciate your helping us out with this?"

Tyrants hate to be defied, but they hate wimps even more. They want you to be respectful, but deep down they want to know you've got some guts.

Conveniently for everyone, that's exactly how you should act. Be polite, but don't be intimidated. Don't grab your father by the collar and snarl, "Listen, old man, you watch your tone of voice, or you'll be moving this furniture all by yourself." But don't cringe and take whatever Daddy dishes out.

Barbara, married with two teenagers, said, "I was thirty-seven years old before I stood up to my father. Dad was rattling on and on about how awful teenagers are today, and I just couldn't take it anymore. My children are good kids, and so are their friends, and I get tired of my father basing his opinions on the horror stories he reads in the newspaper. So, in the middle of his speech, I said, 'You don't know what you're talking about, Dad.'

"He stopped in midsentence and slowly said, 'What?'—as if he couldn't believe his ears. So I said, 'You're wrong. You're just plain wrong, and I don't intend to listen to it.'

"There was a long silence, and then he said, 'Oh,' and changed the subject. I think it shocked me as much as it did him. Strangely enough, we've gotten along much better since then. I think he realized I wasn't quite the doormat he thought I was."

THE BULLY

"You'll Do It Our Way, or Else..."

Bullies go one step beyond intimidation; they actually threaten you.

- "If you invite your father and his new wife to your wedding," one divorced mother told her son, "you can count on me not being there."

- "I won't stand for my daughter living in sin," one father said. "You either get married or move into your own apartment—or you won't be welcome in our house."

- "If you marry that loser, we'll never speak to you again."

Bullies have no interest in what you want, what's best for you, or what would make you happy. They are only interested in what *they* want. And they are willing to disown you, if that's what it takes, to get their way.

Don't Deal with Blackmailers

There is one and only one way to react to threats from your parents: Call their bluff. The appropriate replies to the above three scenarios are, respectively:

- "I'm sorry you're unhappy about it, but I am going to invite my father and his new wife to my wedding. I hope you'll come anyway, but if you don't, I'll understand."

- "I know it upsets you that I'm living with someone, but I'm an adult now, and I have the right to live my life my way. If you choose to break off our relationship because of it, that's your right. But I hope you won't do that."

- "I've listened to what you had to say about my fiancé, and I understand your concerns. But I also intend to get married. Whether you speak to me again or not is your decision, not mine."

Bullies try to hand *you* the decision on whether or not they go through with their threat. Don't take it. In fact, hand it back. Decide how you want to handle the situation, and then tell them it's *their* move.

Since threats can all too easily blow up into family feuds that last for years, react calmly ("I'm sorry you feel that way") and sympathetically ("I can understand why you're upset"). And always give them a face-saving way out ("For my sake, I really hope you won't do that").

But don't give in. Once a Bully knows that threats work, there will be no end to the ultimatums.

When Threats Become Reality

If your parents do decide to never speak to you again, listen to the message they're sending you. They are telling you that getting their own way is more important than having a relationship with you.

So before you get all upset that they don't love you anymore, think about it. *Getting their way is more important to them than you are.* They'd rather not talk to you than give up control of the situation.

Not very flattering, is it?

Maybe you're not as important to them as you think you are—or as they claim you are.

Once you have seen it from this perspective, it shouldn't bother you as much. Take the following two-step approach:

Make a few attempts to patch it up. Tell your parents that you're sorry they're upset, but that it's not worth destroying the relationship over. Do *not* apologize for your actions, and don't give in. But don't ask them for an apology, either. Saying "I'm sorry" doesn't come easy for Bullies.

Make at least three attempts to patch it up. But don't beg. Maintain a "Let's be reasonable" attitude toward the problem.

Wait them out. If your parents still won't budge, give it up. When they are ready to talk to you again, they will. Continue to send cards and presents on birthdays and holidays (as if nothing were wrong) to emphasize how petty they're being—and to give them an opening to talk to you.

But other than that, don't worry about it. A few months off without talking to your parents will probably be quite enjoyable.

And it's the only way to teach them they can't bully you.

7

The Inattentive, the Distracted, and the Oblivious

DINNER IS almost over at your parents' house. Your mother scrapes up the last crumbs of angel food cake and stuffs them into your mouth. You sip bravely at your coffee, which is 415 degrees Fahrenheit and so strong you could use it for oven cleaner. You watch your mother move relentlessly between the kitchen and the dining room, clearing plates, putting away food, pouring coffee, and all the while emitting a steady stream of conversation. But she's not talking to you; she's just talking.

Your father, who had one ear and one eye on the television throughout dinner, gets up without so much as a "Good dinner, dear" to your mother, a "Nice to see you, kid" to you, or an "Excuse me" to anybody, and relocates to the living room to watch TV.

Your mother never breaks stride—in words or steps. If, like your dad, you got up and walked out, the monologue would continue unabated. She picks up your coffee cup, wipes off the table, says, "Don't get up, don't get up," and retreats to the kitchen to do the dishes.

You sit in the empty dining room with the feeling that your parents aren't fully aware you're here. What they *are* focused on isn't clear. It may be an episode of "Dallas," what the neighbors are doing, or cosmic rays from outer space. It's hard to tell.

But whatever they're paying attention to, it isn't you.

Silently, you wait. Maybe they'll come back. Maybe they'll realize you went to a lot of effort to be here for dinner. Maybe Rod Serling will appear and clear up your confusion. Maybe he'll tell you that you only *think* you had dinner with your parents, when actually you've been eating in . . . The Parent Zone.

HOW TO COPE WITH PARENTS WHO HAVE LOST TOUCH

The Inattentive, the Distracted, and the Oblivious are an array of parents who aren't securely connected to reality. They're off in their own little worlds, doing their own little things. They're on automatic pilot—destination unknown.

The common thread with these parents is that you can't get through to them. It's as if you're invisible—which can be frustrating if for some reason you're trying to get their attention. Most of these parents aren't vicious or nasty or manipulative; they're just goofy. But a goofy parent is at least a happy parent—and, as we saw in the previous chapter, things could be worse.

To deal with these folks, you need a large reservoir of patience and understanding. You have to let them do their own thing, as we authors raised in the sixties like to say, while you do yours. Accept the fact that you can't straighten them out, you can't get them back in touch with planet Earth, and you can't get them interested in anything they have decided to ignore—even if that's you.

So let's talk about how to keep the following parent types from putting you in a rubber room: the Jabberer, the Repeater, the Disorganized, the Over-Organized, the Self-Centered, and the Escapist.

THE JABBERER

*"YourUncleBobHasANewJob,AndDidYouKnowEthel's
DaughterIsHomeForTheHolidays,Too? HowDoYouLike
OurNewRecliner? IHadToGoToEightStoresBefore
IFoundAColorThatMatchedTheCarpet.OfCourse,
ThisCarpetIsFifteenYearsOld,But . . ."*

Something strange happens to people who have been married a long time. When they're twenty-five, the husband does all the talking, and the wife is too shy to say anything. When they're sixty-five, the wife is doing five thousand words a minute, and the husband only grunts once every three weeks.

In order to keep up this five-thousand-words-a-minute pace, your mother has to cover some very broad ground.

She tells you, in excruciating detail, what happened to people you went to elementary school, junior high school, and high school with. Not the people you'd like to hear about, like your junior prom date, the math genius you had a crush on, or your former best friend. No, she tells you about the kids you didn't hang around with and don't remember now. Harold Eggbert—"His mother said he was in your senior English class," your mother says indignantly, "what do you mean you don't remember him?"—now owns a used-car lot in New Jersey. And somebody who was in your health class—or maybe she was a year behind you—but your mother can't remember her name—is pregnant with her fifth baby.

Then she describes at stupefying length what the new supermarket looks like: They've got food in barrels, of all things, and lawn furniture, and it's simply amazing; you'll have to take a tour of it before you leave. But you have to bag your own groceries, so of course your father refuses to shop there. "'At those prices,'" she says that he says, "'they've got a hell of a nerve telling me to pack up my own groceries.'"

If you take her anywhere in a car, she reads to you: road signs, street signs, billboards, names of businesses, and all bumper stickers. She tells you who lives in each house you drive by, what the inhabitants do for a living, how many kids they have, and how you can expect them or their kids to act if you happen to run into them at the new supermarket while you're here.

When your eyes glaze over, your jaw goes slack, and drool begins to run down your chin, she will discuss how tired you look and speculate at length on the possible causes of your fatigue—none of which, of course, include her.

There Is No Escape

Attempts to switch Mom over to more meaningful or interesting topics of conversation are ineffective. If you bring up the latest airline hijacking in the Middle East, all she says is "Isn't that awful?"

But the subject of hijackings does remind her of her friend Margaret, who told her how awful the high school students act on the bus these days—why, the bus driver must feel as if *he's* being hijacked! You see, Margaret's daughter is a teacher—that's how she knows about the bus situation—and she has lunchroom duty once a week, and she says those kids are terrorists. That's all they are, terrorists.

This Isn't a Conversation

With Jabberers, you have to understand what you're involved in. Most of you mistakenly believe that:

1. You're in a conversation.

2. You're supposed to be listening.

3. You're supposed to respond.

None of that is true. Jabbering is no more conversation than whistling or nail-biting is. It's simply a nervous habit. You don't have to react to it. You don't have to act interested, nod, ask questions that show you're listening, or make any of the other polite gestures you've been taught to use when someone is talking to you. You can turn on the radio, watch television, or excuse yourself to go put a load of laundry in. The Jabberer won't care.

They're like small children. Little kids talk nonstop about anything and everything, and as long as you're in the same room, that's good enough for them. You don't hang on their every word ("That's great, Susie, so then exactly what happened after you roller-skated down the driveway with Jamie and Annie?"); you just let them talk.

Treat adult Jabberers the same way. Just smile at them every sixty to ninety seconds, and they'll be happy.

There's Safety in Numbers

If you really can't stand the mindless drivel, there are a few ways to get some relief.

Stay in a crowd. With other people around, you can get a conversation (a real one) going with someone else, or pawn the Jabberer off on somebody else.

Put the Jabberer into more formal surroundings. A nice restaurant can also help, since Jabberers (like everybody else) become more conscious of their behavior when they're in a more sophisticated environment. But don't put them in an extremely formal setting, or they'll get nervous and really start babbling.

Escape. Go to the store, take a nap, or take a walk. Take a break from them in the hope that, by the time you get back, they will have occupied themselves with something besides talking to you.

Call for a time-out. It sometimes works to ask them to slow down: "Mom, you're all wound up. Why don't we take a little quiet time?"

THE REPEATER

"Did I Ever Tell You About...?"

Another entrant in the Conversational Olympics is the Repeater. Repeaters gather a little audience together and tell stories—not necessarily boring stories or stupid stories, just the same stories, over and over again.

When they start in with "That reminds me of the time our car broke down outside Tuba City, Arizona," people run screaming from the room.

Fathers seem to have a slight edge on mothers in this category, but either way, it's perpetual summer reruns—to the point that you can lip-sync the words with them:

> **DAD:** I can't believe you paid eighteen thousand dollars for that car. Why, I bought my first car—
>
> **YOU:** For only $752, brand spanking new, right off the showroom floor.
>
> **YOUR SPOUSE:** It was a Chevy Club Coupe—the prettiest shade of blue you've ever seen...
>
> **YOUR CHILDREN:** And you've still got the receipt for it upstairs in your desk.
>
> **DAD** (PUZZLED): Have I told you this story before?

Your parents tell the same stories over and over again because:

1. They like to think and talk about the past: the good old days when they were younger, stronger, better looking, more active, and everything cost less.

2. Nothing new has happened in the old-and-slow lane since the last time they saw you.

3. They want to entertain you, but they've only got a limited number of entertaining stories.

With that in mind, strive for a little tolerance. Repeaters want to have a nice talk with you—it's just that their conversational skills are a little underdeveloped. You've probably repeated *your*self on occasion—though as a friend of mine says, people are much happier *telling* a story twice than *listening* to it twice.

But if you really can't bear to sit through your father's "how-I-got-the-hardware-store-to-give-me-a-free-gallon-of-paint" story again, you can, if you're careful, shut a Repeater off without hurting his or her feelings.

Before Dad gets into great detail about how the clerk mixed the wrong color not once, but twice, and he had to drive down to the store not once, but twice—break in with "Is that the time they gave you a free gallon of paint?" Say it quizzically, as if you *might* have heard this story before—but only once and a long time ago.

Since this takes the wind out of a Repeater's sails—Dad was all geared up to tell you this fascinating story—give him the "great story" reaction he wants: "Boy, you really handled that guy, didn't you?"

Then *slightly* change the subject: "Mom said you were thinking about wallpapering the living room, instead of painting again." Don't switch from painting to getting braces for little Jimmy's teeth, or your father will think you're not interested in these stories he cherishes.

Beat Them to the Punch

Not all Repeaters are storytellers; some just feel the need to supply you with the same information or instructions a hundred zillion times. One daughter said:

"My parents let us use their cabin in the mountains, and we usually spend three or four weekends up there every summer.

Every time we stop by my parents' house to pick up the key, my father tells me that if I lose it on the way up (like it's going to fall out of the car?) or lose it while we're up there, there's an extra set of keys between the fourth and fifth logs from the left on the bottom row of the woodpile. Then he reminds me that the padlock on the door is very stiff, and I'll have to pull down real hard on the lock to get it open.

"He tells me all this several times before we leave, and as we're pulling out of the driveway, he's yelling, 'The extra key is in the woodpile, between the fourth and fifth logs'—while we're driving away with our fingers in our ears."

To be fair to your parents, they do this partly because of all the years you replied, "Yeah, yeah" and meant "I'm not listening to a word you say." And they do it partly because *they* aren't listening to what they say, and they can't remember whether or not they've mentioned it before.

Stave off repetitive advice by giving it first yourself. As soon as you see your father, say, "Okay, Dad, let me see if I remember this right. The extra key is between the fourth and fifth logs from the left on the bottom row of the woodpile. Right?"

If he still beats you to the punch, interrupt him as soon as he gets started and say, "Wait! Don't finish that. Let me see if I remember this right: The extra key is between..."

Tease your father a little about how he doesn't trust your memory. Maybe he'll get the hint that your memory isn't quite as defective as he thinks it is.

THE DISORGANIZED

"Let's See, It Was Here Just a Minute Ago. Or Maybe It Wasn't. I'm Not Sure."

I once saw a greeting card that said, "Life isn't easy for the organizationally impaired."

Well, it's no bed of roses for the people who have to deal with them, either.

It is not amusing to hear your mother—who has never managed to make a grocery list any human being, including herself, could understand—say for the fourth time in one day, "Oh, dear, I forgot something when I went shopping. Would you be a sweetheart and run down to the store and get it for me?"

Nor is it enjoyable to watch your father spend fifteen minutes looking for a screwdriver, while your two-year-old, who has locked himself in the bathroom, screams himself silly.

They're hopeless. It would take Jeane Dixon to find their car keys. Their battery-operated knife sharpener has never been used because they never bought batteries for it. They have the only washer and dryer in town that can't be used simultaneously because of a fuse that burned out when you were in high school.

Give It Up

You can't change the Disorganized. All you can do is protect yourself from them.

1. Do not buy your parents anything that requires assembly, maintenance, better than a third-grade education to operate, or, as previously mentioned, batteries.

2. Show up at your parents' house with the same expectations you'd have upon arriving at a house that hadn't been lived in for thirty years. That way, when they don't have enough food, toilet paper, sheets, or hot water for everyone, you won't be disappointed.

3. For your own safety, do a complete systems check on any major appliance before you use it—particularly their car. Before you drive it or even agree to ride in it, ask: Does it have gas, oil, water, tires?

4. Expect everything to go wrong, and when it does, don't count on any contingency plans or help from your parents.

It's Out of Your Control

Accept your parents for what they are—befuddled by life. Have no expectations of them, and you won't be disappointed.

Paul cautioned, warned, and even threatened his parents about their back porch steps, which were nearly rotted through on one side. It was only a matter of time before a step gave out and somebody broke an ankle or a leg or worse.

His parents were well aware of the danger. Every time someone went out the back door, they'd say, "Be careful on those steps—the boards aren't very sturdy."

But whenever Paul complained about it, all he got was a vague "Yes, we really need to do something about that." And they did nothing.

Unless Paul wants to fix the steps himself, he, like the frustrated offspring of any Disorganized parents, can do only one thing: Shut up.

Nagging never got a Disorganized parent to do anything —no matter how life-threatening the problem. Whether it's fixing rotten steps or seeing a doctor about chest pains, the Disorganized will do it when they're good and ready— which is invariably later rather than sooner, and may be never.

Since your parents have the right to live life as they see fit, you're obligated to leave them alone. As cruel as it sounds, it's their right to fall down the stairs or drop dead of a heart attack. You can't control them.

The only hope you have—and that's a slim one—is to appeal to their concern not for themselves, but for your other parent:

"Dad, by not fixing those steps, you're putting *Mom* in danger. If she falls down those steps, she'll break a hip—or worse. She'll be in the hospital for weeks or months—if a fall like that doesn't kill her, that is."

or

"Mom, I know you don't think those chest pains are serious, but Dad's really worried. *He's* going to have a heart attack if you don't go to a doctor pretty soon."

THE OVERORGANIZED

"We Can Whip This Place into Shape in No Time."

Even more annoying than the Disorganized are the Overorganized. They're determined to revamp you, your family, your house, your yard, and your entire neighborhood, if it's the last thing they ever do.

"My father is my self-appointed maintenance man," Brenda said. "The last time he visited, he wasn't here an hour before he went to the garage for some hedge trimmers and started working on the bushes around the house.

"Then he wanted me to help: 'Brenda, come out here and see if I'm cutting these branches evenly.' When I went outside, he told me to re-edge the lawn, because it was crooked, while he finished the shrubbery.

"It was like that for a week. I couldn't wait for him to go home so I could get some rest."

"My parents believe I'm incapable of feeding myself properly," said Jennifer, a single woman of twenty-seven who—as far as her parents are concerned—has barely left the nest. "When they visit, they bring tons of food: fresh fruit, canned goods, and casseroles my mother's been baking for days.

"My father throws out anything he thinks I shouldn't be eating. He once pulled a carton of yogurt out of the refrigerator and said, 'Nobody should eat this crap,' then dropped it in the trash can."

Home Field Advantage

In your parents' house, there's not much you can do about the Overorganized. You have to give in, the way you did as a child, and vacuum the carpet every time you walk on it, or be ready to leave promptly at 6:57 to make your 7:30 dinner reservations.

But in your own house, you have the right to set the rules.

If it bothers you that your mother starts cleaning the minute she walks in your front door, or that your father keeps overhauling your dishwasher, tell them to stop.

You can say, "I know I'm not much of a housekeeper or a groundskeeper, but I don't want you to do anything about it, and I don't want you to hassle me about it."

That won't necessarily stop them, though, because the Overorganized are tenacious buggers. If you tell your father not to clean out your garage, he'll "just pick up a few things" for you. If you make him quit doing that, he'll stand in the driveway shaking his head and saying, "You'll have to pull the car in yourself. I could never get it in there without hitting something. You probably don't have more than four inches of free space on either side of the car. But don't worry, I'm not going to say anything about what a mess it is. It's your garage—you can do whatever you want to with it."

Gee, thanks, Dad.

Expect that it may take months, if not years, of politely but continually asking the Overorganized to quit harassing you before they actually do quit.

Go with the Flow

But there's another way to look at this: The Overorganized can be a great source of free labor. If your mother wants to arrive with a dust mop and a can of Lemon Pledge in her hand, let her clean to her heart's content. If your father wants to jackhammer up your driveway and lay a new one, more power to him.

Don't take it as a commentary on your inability to run your own home, because it isn't one. Your mother would find dirt in a freshly scrubbed operating room ("I don't know, it *looks* clean, but...."), and your father would find a way to improve the Pebble Beach golf course ("too many trees by the ninth green, I think").

It's not a personal insult; it's a compulsion. So let them compulse. They'll be happy, they'll be out of your hair (as long as you don't let them drag you into it, like Brenda did), and you might even get a new driveway out of it.

THE SELF-CENTERED

"It's Nice that You Got Promoted, but Did We Tell You What We're Doing This Summer?"

The Self-Centered have only one topic of conversation: themselves. If the conversation gets off that topic for more than thirty seconds, they get antsy. When you talk about yourself or your kids or acid rain or the Yankees, your parents begin to drift away. They sigh. They look around the room, hoping someone will walk in and change the subject back to *them*.

If you ignore these little hints—which mean "I can't stand this much longer, you're not talking about Me"— they begin tapping their fingers on the table, looking at their watches, stretching back in their chairs, yawning, picking imaginary lint off their sleeves, until, unable to control themselves, one of them breaks in with "Before you finish that story, did I tell you about what I did yesterday?"

The Self-Centered are brilliant at twisting any conversation around so that it focuses on them.

YOU: Little Jimmy starts first grade in two weeks. It's hard to believe he's that grown-up already.

THE SELF-CENTERED: You know, I've been thinking about going back to school myself. The community college has a writing course I'd like to take. I've always wanted to write a book. I could write the story of my life—what a book that would make! The only problem would be, with all the experiences I've had, the book would have to be about eight hundred pages long.

or

YOU: I've been thinking about looking for another job. I just don't feel appreciated at Global Computer.

THE SELF-CENTERED: That reminds me—I just had my annual review at Universal Thyroid. My boss, who's a vice president now, told me I could fill out the evaluation form myself. He said I'm doing such a good job that he probably couldn't come up with enough superlatives. He thought I'd be able to think up a few.

Don't Call Us, We'll Call You

The sad truth is that Self-Centered parents aren't interested in you. I don't mean they don't care. They do care; they want to know you're healthy and happy. They just don't want you taking up too much of their time.

The Self-Centered parents have their own lives, which don't include you. Being a parent was a nice experience for the Self-Centered, but it's over now, and they're glad. You're something to talk about with their friends and someone to be with during the holidays, but other than that, they have no big need or desire to spend time with you.

How Do You Deal with This?

Children of Self-Centered parents spend a lot of time fruitlessly trying to get their parents' attention and approval. You want the traditional doting Mom and Dad, but what you have is two people who act as if they're childless.

It may be hard to accept, but you're not going to get the affection you want from them—not now, probably not ever. If you want someone to baby you, to hang breathlessly on your every word, and to sympathize with your every problem, you'll have to look elsewhere—because you can't create interest where there is none.

Your parents have made their choice about what interests them, and it's not you.

So don't let a "Let's exchange birthday cards and Christmas presents every year" relationship with your parents bother you anymore. Stay superficially in touch with them, the way they stay superficially in touch with you, then go have an intense, warm, loving, and involved relationship with your spouse, your children, or even your dog.

It will be much more satisfying.

THE ESCAPIST

"Problems? What Problems? We Don't Have Any Problems in This Family."

Escapists have the same problem as Amplifiers: They can't stand it when anything goes wrong. But Escapists take it one step further. They don't get distraught; they deny. They pretend the problem doesn't exist. They have a carefully constructed, if totally distorted, view of how wonderful their lives are (or should be), and they will fight like hell to keep that fantasy intact.

There are two levels of Escapists: The Level I Escapist

tries to rationalize away problems. The Level II Escapist refuses to even hear about them.

Level I Escapists: The Rose-Colored Glasses

Level I Escapists will try to argue you out of the idea that you're having a problem.

YOU: My marriage isn't working out.
THE LEVEL I ESCAPIST: It can't be anything serious. You two have always been so happy. Put in a little more effort and everything will be fine.

or

YOU: My boss doesn't seem too thrilled with the way I do my job. I'm not sure what's wrong.
THE LEVEL I ESCAPIST: I'll tell you what's wrong: Your boss is what's wrong. He should be thanking God four hundred times a day that he's got you working for him. He couldn't ask for a better employee.

The extent to which Escapists will go to deny problems is astounding, and in some cases, sad.

Rachel was an aspiring actress in Los Angeles. Overwhelmed by her failure to get any acting roles and by the pressure in the entertainment industry to stay trim, she developed bulimia. She got help, and her therapist suggested she tell her mother (who was part of the pressure problem) about her condition.

Rachel returned to her hometown, took her mother out to lunch (a neutral location), and explained her illness.

"What's wrong with that?" was her mother's response. "You have to stay thin; you're an actress."

"Mom," Rachel said incredulously, "this is an *illness.*"

"You don't look sick to me."

"This is a neurosis, a mental problem. I overeat, then I throw up, because I can't handle my problems."

"You don't have any mental problems. Nobody in this family has ever had any mental problems. You're a beautiful, talented girl who's going to be very successful, you'll see. You're making a big deal out of nothing."

It took a conversation with the therapist to convince Rachel's mother that her daughter did indeed have a problem. Even then, she wouldn't discuss it with Rachel other than to say, "Are you feeling any better?" or "Do you need money for your doctor bills?"

Level II Escapists: The Vanishing Act

Level II Escapists, usually fathers, don't have to rationalize problems away, because they don't listen to them in the first place. They don't want to hear that your husband is running around or that your fiancée has three kids and her ex-husband is a drug dealer.

"My ex-wife and I continually fight over my visitation rights with my ten-year-old son," Walt said. "She does everything she can to make it difficult, inconvenient, or even impossible. My father, who's very old-school, finds all of this quite distasteful. He doesn't understand how I could have married someone like Alice in the first place. And he certainly doesn't want to hear about my problems with her.

"If I raise the subject, my father gets up and walks out of the room. Literally. He doesn't say anything; he just leaves. And he won't come back until we're talking about something else."

"Please Don't Let Us Have a Problem"

If you try hard enough, you might get an Escapist to face the truth. But you need to ask yourself what you're looking for.

Do you want emotional support? They may give you

money, lend you a car, or put you up for the night, but don't expect commiseration.

Do you want to talk it out? Escapists are too squeamish; they don't want to hear about all this awful stuff. It's too detrimental to their fantasies.

Do you want solutions? Sorry, but even if they accept that there is a problem, most Escapists won't do anything but hope it goes away.

But This Is Between You and Me

The only problems worth trying to hash out with Escapists are the ones that directly involve the two of you.

Of course, it's difficult to say, "Mom, Dad, we don't seem to be getting along very well. Maybe we ought to talk about what the problem is." Because the response you get is "That's ridiculous. We don't have a problem. The only problem we have is that you *think* we've got a problem."

But you may want to give it a try anyway.

The Effects of the Generation Gap

Our generation believes in "letting it all hang out" (there's another old sixties phrase for you): being honest, expressing our true feelings, and letting other people know what's on our minds.

Our parents were raised entirely differently. Gary Cooper and John Wayne—strong, silent types—were our fathers' role models. A man didn't talk to his wife or his children about love, guilt, happiness, or pain. He kept all that inside and maintained an image of strength and security.

Our mothers patterned themselves after Doris Day and Debbie Reynolds: The way to a man's heart was to look good and not say anything intelligent. A woman was supposed to be the perfect homemaker, companion, and mother. She wasn't supposed to have crying spells or become an alcoholic or need a handful of tranquilizers in order to face the children at breakfast. If she did, it was covered up so the neighbors didn't find out.

Our parents were trained by society to be Escapists. Images were more important than reality. Personal insights and psychological introspection were unheard of. Telling each other what they really thought simply wasn't done.

It's a little late to try to undo that training now.

8

The Visit

THE PHONE RINGS, and it's your mother.

"It's been so long since we've seen you, dear," she says in that saccharine voice that means she wants something. You cringe; you're not going to like what's coming. "I thought I'd fly out next month and visit you for a few weeks."

There's nothing but stunned silence on your end of the line. A few weeks? You groan inwardly. Major dental surgery sounds more appealing.

But what can you do? You can't say, "No, Ma, don't come. Don't visit me, please! You've always wanted me to be happy, and there's no way I can be happy if you're here criticizing my job, my housekeeping, my kids, and how late I stay up at night."

So, like a good, obedient child, you summon up all the emotional fortitude you've got, try to recall the countless Miss Manners columns you've read exhorting you to respect your elders, and with feigned—and strained—politeness, say weakly, "Gee, Mom, that would be, uh, great."

Then inspiration strikes. "But, Mom, you can't leave Dad alone for that long. He'd go crazy without you."

"Oh, don't worry about him," she replies, dismissing him

like so much dust on her African violets. "He's been so busy with his fly-fishing this summer that he's been ignoring me for weeks. I'll be glad to get away from him for a while. Besides, if I'm not here to wait on him hand and foot, maybe he'll remember he *has* a wife."

Nice try. You attempted to stop her with a flimsy excuse (granted it was the only one you could think of on such short notice), but it didn't work. And now it's too late to use a better excuse, one she might not argue with, like "Mom, I'm being evicted from my apartment next week."

You're trapped. She's coming to visit, and she's coming to visit for a *long* time.

By the end of that "few weeks" visit, you and your spouse are at each other's throats, your children are spending all their time hiding in their rooms, and you know that if you never see your mother again as long as both you and she live, it will be too soon.

That Trapped Feeling

And now you feel guilty. I mean, you love your mother and all, but these visits make you crazy. And there seems to be no good way to stop them. You know that if you tell her *not* to come, or to come only for a few days, her feelings will be hurt. She'll say that you don't love her, that you don't want to see her, that your life is so full of more important things that you don't have time to be bothered with an old woman like her.

Or else she'll fight you on it.

> **YOU:** Mom, we'd love to have you, but I've just started this new job, so I'm at the office late almost every night, and little Jimmy has football practice three times a week, and— well, we just couldn't give you the attention you deserve. You'd end up spending most of your time alone. Maybe another time would be better....
>
> **MOM:** Nonsense, dear, that's just what I need: some time

alone. I just want to sit and relax. I don't expect to be treated like a guest in my own child's house. Besides, it sounds as if you could use some help. I can take care of the house while you're working and pick up little Jimmy from football practice. You'll see, it'll be perfect.

It may be perfect for you, Mom, but it certainly isn't going to be perfect for me.

> **YOU:** Well, okay, but with all that we've got going on, it might be better if you only stayed a week. Things are pretty hectic right now and—
>
> **MOM:** Fly from Seattle to Dallas, and only stay a week? You must be joking. It would hardly be worth the trip. Do you have any idea how high airfares are these days? I've already bought my ticket, and let me tell you, it cost me an arm and a leg. Why, when *my* mother used to visit, she'd stay for *two months*.

The thought of your mother visiting for two months renders you temporarily (and perhaps permanently) speechless, and you're stuck again.

Whose Fault Is This?

While you're nodding your head in dismayed agreement, stop and ask yourself whose fault it is that you get stuck like this.

"What do you mean?" you say with surprise. "My mother loves me and wants to visit me so she can bask in the warmth and charm of my wonderful personality, and if I turn her down, she'll be heartbroken."

I see. And that's why she's going to barge in on you un-invited and make your life miserable for weeks on end?

Stop kidding yourself. Your mother *acting* heartbroken and your mother *being* heartbroken are two very different things.

That's not to say that she *doesn't* want to see you. All

parents (well, almost all parents) enjoy seeing their children. Your parents want to know that your life is going well, that you are happy, that they did a good, competent job of raising you, and that despite the rough spots, you turned out to be a decent human being. But emotionally destroyed if this visit doesn't come off? Not hardly.

No, this visit is happening for several other reasons. As she said, your mother wants to get away from your father for a while so she can teach him a lesson about ignoring her. She wants a vacation so she can "just sit back and relax." Since she's going alone on this "vacation," she wants to go where she knows someone (like you). And she wants to go where the room rates are the lowest.

Most of all, this visit is being governed by The Three Laws of Parental Visitation. These are among the most long-standing, inflexible, unchanging rules of parent-child relations (regardless of the ages of those parents and children), and parents hold them sacred.

THE LAWS OF PARENTAL VISITATION

1. Parents and their emancipated children *must* visit each other. Whether or not they enjoy those visits is irrelevant.

2. Children want to see their parents. In fact, your parents assume that there is no limit to your wanting to see them. If nothing else, they're convinced that you *should* want to see them, after all they've done for you.

3. The length of your parents' visit must be in direct proportion to how far they had to travel and how much money they had to spend to get there. If you live next door, your mother may be satisfied with a half-hour visit. If you live in Hong Kong, she will spend the better part of a year with you.

   Even in this day of 5-hour flights from New York to Los Angeles and $299 airfares, it simply isn't economically sound, morally right, or psychologically possible for your parents to go that far and stay for just the weekend.

Behold the generation gap.

People of our generation think nothing of traveling across the country for a few days' visit, whether it's business, pleasure, or to see relatives (which is different from traveling for pleasure). It's done all the time. But people in our parents' generation don't see it that way. They remember when cross-country travel was a major expedition: expensive, time-consuming, dirty, dusty, and a real strain on the family budget. And they still think of it that way.

You and your parents may have absolutely nothing to say to each other after the first two hours, but that won't stop them from staying for another two weeks.

"But You're Not Our Friend, You're Our Child"

Your parents wouldn't dream of calling their friends, telling them they're coming for a visit, and informing them that they're going to stay for three weeks, because

1. Their friends are adults.
2. Adults don't treat each other that way.
3. Your parents know it.

Friends arrange for a visit like this:

YOUR MOTHER (HINTING): I could certainly use some time away from here. Harry has been driving me crazy with this fishing business. The man hardly knows I'm alive.

HER FRIEND: I've got a great idea. Why don't you come out and stay with us for a few days?

YOUR MOTHER (PRETENDING TO BE SURPRISED): That *is* a great idea. But no, I couldn't possibly impose on you like that. I'd just be in the way.

HER FRIEND: Don't be silly—you wouldn't be in the way. We'd love to have you.

YOUR MOTHER: Okay, but only for a few days. I know how busy you always are.

HER FRIEND: Great. Why don't you fly out next Friday and stay the weekend with us?

YOUR MOTHER: I'll make the reservations, and call you back tomorrow.

Why, you may be asking yourself, doesn't it ever work this way when your mother is calling *you?* It doesn't work that way for several reasons:

1. You are not your parents' friend; you are their child.

2. Your parents are not in the habit of being courteous to you.

3. You never invite your parents to visit; you force them to invite themselves.

That's Not a Request; That's an Order

Your mother (if she's like most parents) doesn't *ask* your permission to visit; she *tells* you she's coming. She refuses to acknowledge that you have your own family, your own home, and your own life. You're not an adult friend; you're her *child.* You're part of *her* family. When it's convenient or desirable *from her standpoint* to visit you, she calls up and announces that she's coming.

To many parents, your house is an extension of the old family home—the same way you are an extension of them. During your childhood, your mother didn't hesitate to go into your room to get your dirty laundry or to put your toys away. She certainly didn't wait for an invitation. And today she still doesn't hesitate to go into your "room"—without an invitation—even though that room is a 2,500-square-foot house that's 780 miles away. All you get is a perfunctory "knock on the door" to let you know she's on her way in.

The Correct Answer Is "Yes," "Yes," or "Yes"

She may couch the announcement in superficially polite terms, such as "I thought, if it was all right with you, that I'd come to visit for a couple of weeks in October" or "What would you think about my coming out to see you in April?" But this display of "manners" is just that: a display of manners. She's not asking you a real question that can be answered yes or no.

Parents who preface a request with "Would you mind..." expect you to grant their request—no matter what they are asking you for. Your mother doesn't expect you to say no when she "asks" to come for a visit. Your father doesn't expect you to say no when he "asks" you to run down to the corner grocery store and buy him some chocolate milk.

"Would you mind..." is not a question. It is a polite way of giving you an order. Any time your parents say, "Would you mind...", all they want to hear you say is "Fine," "Great," "Wonderful," "Be glad to," or "What a marvelous suggestion."

Your parents don't ask permission to visit you, because *they never ask your permission about anything else, and they never have.* They didn't when you were five years old, and they are not about to start now.

Taking the Reins

It's time to take your life out of your parents' hands and put it where it belongs: in your hands. There's no reason to let your parents run your life—or *ruin* your life—for a few weeks, a few days, or even a few hours.

The problem is that you are acting out of blind habit. Thanks to years of childhood conditioning, it "feels" better to do what your parents want than to do what you want. It has become second nature to do it their way.

But you're an adult. It's ridiculous to be controlled by your parents in your thirties and forties simply because of what they taught you when you were five or ten years old. It's ridiculous, because your parents no longer have any real power over you. The only power they have is the power you give them.

If you don't believe that, ask yourself, "What's the worst that can happen?" What will happen if you tell your mother to stay one week instead of "a few weeks"?

She'll be mad? Your mother has been mad at you before. She'll get over it now, just as she's gotten over it in the past.

She'll be so mad that she'll decide to make you miserable? She'll tell you off, write you nasty letters, call daily and complain about how badly you treat her? Maybe. But she'll give up these little games if she doesn't get any emotional return for terrorizing you.

Don't beg for forgiveness or get mad and yell back. Just maintain a firm but polite attitude (you're positive you want to see her, but you're positive you don't want to see her for that long a period of time) and she'll realize her tirades are useless.

She'll never speak to you again? Doubtful. If you don't grovel, it will take longer for her to come around, but she will eventually. If she doesn't, then you're dealing with a person who would rather have her own way than have a relationship with you, and, frankly, you're not losing much.

The bottom line is that if you start doing things *your* way, the world won't come to an end.

Sacrificing your happiness, your peace of mind, and the sanity of your household so your parents won't be displeased is nonsensical. Don't do it. You are an adult, and adults control their own lives. They don't let other people control their lives for them.

Do things *your* way. Make yourself happy, and let the parental chips fall where they may.

How to Have It Your Way
(Without Starting World War III)

Ohmigod, you're thinking. If my mother calls and says she's coming to visit for three weeks and I say, "No way," the fight is on.

In an ideal world, you could explain to your parents that a three-week visit isn't in the best interest of the relationship:

> "I love you very much, and I enjoy seeing you, but these long visits seem to wear everybody down. Don't you agree? We feel cramped; the house is too small for us even when we don't have company. And I know that the kids get on your nerves. So why don't you come for three days instead of three weeks, and that way we can make it 'quality time' and not have anyone be uncomfortable."

In this ideal world, your mother would reply graciously:

> "I understand, dear. I hate to admit it, but I agree that a short visit would probably be better. That doesn't mean that I don't love you. We each just have our own way of doing things, and problems occur when we have to adjust our respective life-styles for an extended period of time."

Right. If you had that kind of relationship with your parents, you wouldn't be reading this book.

In the real world, Mom's reaction is more like:

> "*My* visits wear *you* down? You feel *cramped* with me in the house? Well, you don't ever have to worry about getting worn down or being cramped again, because as far as I'm concerned, you and that bum you married and my poor unfortunate grandchildren who have to have such selfish parents as you two can go straight to . . ."

That's the problem with the "ideal world" approach: You usually don't get an "ideal world" reaction. In the real world, at least initially, it may be better to *manage* the problem instead of confronting it. It may be better to apply subtle but steady pressure on your parents and "retrain" them, because it involves less confrontation and less emotional stress. It doesn't force your parents to react; it merely encourages them to cooperate and go along with *your* program.

Jump Right in There

The key to managing the visitation problem (and most other problems) is to take control immediately. The sooner you take responsibility, the greater the chances that the outcome will go your way. The longer you leave the situation in your parents' hands, the worse it gets.

Elaine had recently started a consulting business and was working out of her home, when her mother, who lived several states away, called and "asked" if she could come to visit. Elaine reluctantly agreed, but put off talking about when and for how long, hoping her mother would forget about it. In less than a week she received a letter from her mother stating, "I'll be there from the seventh to the twenty-first of next month."

Elaine couldn't believe it. She was having trouble getting her business off the ground; her husband wasn't happy about the fact that her clients, knowing her office was in her home, called her evenings and weekends; and since it was summer, her kids were underfoot all day, taking up time she should have been spending on work. And now her mother was going to descend on her for two weeks.

The pressure was too much. Elaine decided she had to cancel this visit or at least shorten it considerably. She called her mother and tried to talk her out of coming. She said that she was busy and wouldn't be able to spend much time with her, that she was under a strain trying to get her business going, that the kids were being a pain. Naturally, her mother had an answer for everything: She could get along fine by herself; she could keep house for Elaine and baby-sit the kids. No problem, no problem.

Finally, in desperation, Elaine said, "Mother, I just think it would be better if you didn't stay that long."

"Fine," her mother said icily, and hung up.

Three days later, Elaine got another letter from her mother. This one announced that since obviously Elaine didn't want to see her, she could forget about her *ever* coming to visit.

Elaine immediately called to apologize, but her mother refused to come to the phone. So Elaine wrote to her, begging her to visit, but got no reply. After several more phone calls, Elaine finally talked her mother into visiting—on her mother's original schedule, of course—and was not only stuck with the visit but had to cater to her mother's hurt feelings and listen to her mother's constant complaining about what an ingrate Elaine was.

Elaine's mother may have been pushy, insensitive, selfish, and manipulative, but she wasn't totally at fault. Elaine brought this problem on herself by handling the situation all wrong. She didn't take control when she had the chance, and she was afraid to stand up to her mother once her mother started pushing her around emotionally.

Elaine failed to follow the Rules of Visit Management.

THE RULES OF VISIT MANAGEMENT

1. Never accept the idea, the suggestion, or even the hint of a visit without immediately stating *your* preferences about when and for how long.

2. Always give irrefutable, unarguable reasons why the visit has to be the way *you* want it to be.

3. When negotiating the terms of a visit, always make closed-end, specific suggestions that require a yes-or-no answer. Fight the decades of conditioning that make you want to say, "What would be best for you?"

Rule #1: State Your Preferences

When you hear your mother or father say, "We thought we'd come out and visit you next month," respond swiftly with:

> "Terrific! The twentieth through the twenty-fourth would be perfect for me."

If your parent starts out more specifically with something like "I'm coming to visit for three weeks next month," say:

> "I can't wait to see you, but I just don't know how I can work out the three-week part—not next month, anyway."

Don't stop here, or your parents will want to know "Why not?" Continue quickly with:

> "But if you could come from the twentieth to the twenty-seventh, that would work out great. Let me see here [pretend to be looking at a calendar], yes, the week of the twentieth would be super. I know that's less time than you'd planned to spend, but I'd hate to put it off until later in the summer. What do you say? Is the week of the twentieth okay?"

Avoid making excuses. Just tell them their visit at that particular time would be inconvenient, and suggest alternate dates. Focus on the time and duration of the visit rather than the reasons you want to change it.

Rule #2: Give Unarguable Reasons

If they still want to know why three weeks won't work, then give them excuses. But make them solid. Elaine got herself in trouble by giving her mother vague excuses that could be easily countered. Don't give your parents room to maneuver by offering weak, ineffectual reasons for rearranging or postponing their visit.

A WEAK EXCUSE	YOUR PARENTS' RESPONSE
There's not enough room.	The couch will be fine.
I've really got my hands full right now.	We don't need any of your time. We can entertain ourselves. or We'll come out and take some of the load off you.
The kids have the flu.	You had the flu all the time when you were little. We never caught it then, and I'm sure we won't catch it now. or I can baby-sit while you're at work.
The house is a wreck.	I'll help you clean it when I get there.
We'll be out of town that week.	Just leave the keys, and we'll be there when you get back.
We're getting a divorce. We haven't spoken to each other for days.	Then you could probably use some company.

Even though these are all perfectly good reasons why you don't want company, your parents won't see it that way. If you tell them the truth—that you're just not up to seeing them or to having *any* house guests right now—they'll be insulted.

So if your parents insist, give them the only excuse they can't argue with: You've got other visitors coming. Whether that's true or not.

In other words, lie.

(If it bothers you to lie to your parents, remember that it's also lying to say you'd be delighted to have them camp out on your sofa bed for a month.)

The goal here is not to relate to your parents through a veil of lies and falsehoods. As I said in chapter 3, it's important to be honest with your parents. But this is an emergency. You've got to reorient their thinking, to make them realize that their visits have to be planned *and agreed upon* in advance by both of you.

So for everyone's sake, say:

> "Pat, my old friend from college, will be here at the same time you're talking about coming. I'm afraid I'm already committed."

Then apply Rule #1, and suggest a new time—one that *you* are comfortable with. Say,

> "Why don't you and Dad plan on coming out and staying over that following weekend?"

Be very specific, so they know you mean the weekend *only:*

> "If you get here Thursday night, I'd still have to work Friday, but we could go out to lunch, and then I'd have all weekend with you. I'll arrange to go to work late on Monday so I can take you to the airport. How does that sound?"

Some parents will be offended that you only want them to stay for a few days, and if they live in Miami and you live in San Francisco, they may have a point. But even if they're driving in from Argentina, a week is plenty. You wouldn't let a friend stay with you for weeks on end; why let your parents?

Rule #3: No Open-Ended Questions

Make all your suggestions easily answered by yes or no, fine or not fine. Don't ask, "When did you want to come?" or "What would be a good time for you?" Name the time, and let them agree or disagree. If they disagree, name another time. And stay at it until you're satisfied with the details.

It is essential that you leave your parents no openings, no chance to launch a counteroffensive. Don't say, "Well, gosh, I'm just not sure," hoping that they'll take the hint and back off. If they have their minds made up, they won't back off an inch. End every response with a concrete suggestion that requires agreement or disagreement.

> **DO SAY:** This weekend's not good? How about the weekend after next?
>
> **DO NOT SAY:** This weekend's not good? Well, then (sigh), when do you want to come?

That's giving them a license to run all over you.

The Counterattack

Back in the ideal world, your parents would respond to the news about Pat's visit—and your suggestion that they come the following weekend—just the way they would to friends their own age. They'd say, "That sounds fine—but are you sure it won't be too much trouble having company two weekends in a row?" (Of course, it won't be too much trouble, because phantom Pat won't be there. You'll have to concoct another story about why Pat couldn't make it at the last minute.)

But in this, the real world, your parents may say a number of things—none of them nearly so cooperative. Don't be surprised at the counterarguments they'll use to keep arrangements the way they had originally planned them:

- "We could stay in a hotel until your company leaves."
- "Your dad's already asked for time off work."
- "We were so sure you wouldn't mind our staying for three weeks that we've already bought our plane tickets."

Last Resorts

In the face of true belligerency, you still have some options.

Appeal to their better nature. Parents rarely exhibit their finer social abilities around their children, but give it a try. Say, "You're really making this difficult. I've already made other plans. Could you help me out by being flexible?"

Point out who's creating this problem. If your parents haven't given you much notice (which is standard operating procedure), diplomatically mention that they've caused this problem: "I had no idea you were planning to come out. I wish you had let me know sooner, so we could have worked something out."

Parents who made plans or bought tickets without consulting you deserve no consideration whatsoever—because they aren't giving you any. Tell them, "I'm sorry, but there's nothing I can do about my other plans. I guess you'll have to trade in your tickets."

Take advantage of any uncertainty. If your parents hesitate when you recommend changes in their visit plans, press your advantage. Enthusiastically encourage them to do it your way: "Oh, come on, it will be fun. I've got this great restaurant I want to take you to. Say you'll come— even though it's only for the weekend."

Threaten to postpone their visit indefinitely. It may force them into accepting your timetable if you say, "It's too bad all this is happening at the same time. But I'd much rather have you stay the weekend *now*, than put this off until sometime in the future when you could stay longer." Use the phrase *sometime in the future* to indicate that as far as you're concerned, it's either now or three years from now.

Say, "Let's postpone it for a few months until things settle down around here. What about the end of April?" Mention a specific month, but make it far off in the distant future. Faced with the choice of now or next year, they may agree to do it your way.

Change their mode of transportation. "Why don't you fly?" Or, if fear of flying is a problem for them, "Why not take the train? It *is* crazy to spend eight days driving round trip in order to spend six days at my house."

Get involved in paying for the visit. The natural response to "Why don't you fly?" is "Because it's too expensive." If you can afford to, jump in and say, "Well, this visit isn't just for you, it's for all of us"—that shows how much you want to see them—"so why don't I pick up half of the airfare?" Or all of the airfare, if you can handle it. Then add, "I'll even make the reservations for you." That way you can control exactly when they arrive and when they leave.

Encourage your parents to make visiting you a part of their vacation, instead of all of their vacation. If you live in Richmond, suggest that your parents stay with you for two or three days on their way to Virginia Beach—and another couple of days on their way back—instead of spending all ten days of their vacation at your place.

Turn the tables and arrange to visit them. Say, in a pleasant, cooperative, adult tone of voice: "You're right. This trip is going to be really inconvenient for you. So instead of you putting out all the effort, why don't I fly down there for that weekend?"

Stand and fight. Depending on how pushy your parents are—and how fed up you get—you may want to take off the gloves and get down to some serious scrapping. Only you can decide how far you want to push it the first time around. But slow and easy is the most prudent course of action. A moderate show of resistance this time may open the door to your gaining complete control of the next visit. Remember, this is only the opening battle in a long war to get control of your life.

PREVENTIVE MEDICINE

Once you get over the crisis of your parents' impending visit, lay some groundwork so the crisis won't happen again.

Parents are not like friends, casual acquaintances, or even enemies. They won't go away. And, like it or not, you are tied to these people for the rest of your—or their—lives. Unless you are willing to sever the relationship or curtail it dramatically, you have to continue to see them.

But it doesn't have to be the long, drawn-out misery it has been in the past. You can make the whole situation more palatable by putting these preventive measures into action:

Invite your parents to visit. That may be the last thing you want to do, but inviting your parents for a visit puts you in the driver's seat. You can invite them for the amount of time you want, for the dates you want. Extending an invitation assures them that you do love them, that you do want to see them, that you are a good son or daughter, that your spouse doesn't really hate them—and it lessens the emotional pressure they feel to show up on your doorstep to see if you still care.

When your parents hint that they'd like to visit, don't change the subject. Decide when *you* would like to see them, and extend an invitation.

Visit your parents before they can visit you. If you really can't bear the thought of your parents in your house, or you can't get their visits under control, go to your parents before they can come to you. When you visit them on a regular basis—even if that basis isn't as often as they'd like

—your parents will be less inclined to make the pilgrimage to your house. Even stopping over for an evening during a business trip may be enough, if you do it several times a year.

Discuss the next visit before the current one ends. The single biggest cause of parents nagging you about visiting them—or showing up at your house uninvited—is that they don't know when they are going to see you again. End every visit by arranging the next one. Say, "It will probably be spring before we can get back out here" or "Why don't you two think about coming back next summer for a week?"

Don't give your parents time to sit around their kitchen table discussing when they should drive out to see you again. You won't like their decision.

THE PARENTS NEXT DOOR

The rules of Visit Management apply even to parents who live two blocks from you—maybe even more so, since they have the ability to drop in forty-three times a day.

When parents who abuse their visiting privileges show up at the door, don't feel obligated to drop everything and sit for an hour and chat. Instead say, "Gosh, I wish I had known you were going to stop over. I'm just on my way out the door to go to the store"—or the post office, or the bank, or whatever excuse is convenient. "Why don't I call you when I get back?" And usher them gently out the door.

Then do call. Don't make commitments and then not live up to them, or your parents will become even more relentless in their attempts to see you. If you've been remiss in the past, using "I'll call you later" as an excuse to get rid of them, and then *not* calling them back, you have a few promises to live up to before your parents will trust you again.

But don't hesitate to cut that call short if you're busy. And forestall another unannounced visit by ending your call with a statement like "Today has been kind of hectic. Why don't I call you back at the end of the week?" Or "Why don't I come over Saturday afternoon about three o'clock, when I can give you my undivided attention?"

It will take work and persistence to reeducate your parents that your sole function in life is not to help them pass the time. If they can't wait until the end of the week but call the next day, act surprised and say pleasantly, "But I told you I'd call you at the end of the week. And I will. I'm afraid today isn't any better than yesterday was. I'll call you for sure on Friday."

If they don't call, but stop by again, don't give in. Give another excuse, like "I have to go to the bank," and hustle the persistent parent out the door.

If your parents are skeptical about your having to run errands, ask them to come along. Then drag them to the bank, the supermarket, the dry cleaner, and anywhere else you can think to go. Don't slow down for them, don't ask them where they would like to go, and once you're on the road, don't ask them if they mind if you make one more stop—in fact, make all the stops you can. No one (except children under ten) likes to tag along behind someone who's rushing all over town. Your parents want to sit down with a cup of coffee and talk about their favorite topic of conversation (which is generally different from your favorite topic of conversation). If they can't force you to do that, they'll stop coming by.

A variation on this, if you have no errands to do, is to put your parents to work when they come over. If you're doing the dishes, ask your mother to clear the table and wipe the counters. If you're working on the lawn, ask your father to get out the pruning saw and start working on the elm tree. Unless they're workaholics (and if they are, don't use this tactic—you'll never get rid of them), they'll voluntarily reduce the number of times they come knocking on your door.

Don't feel bad about asking an old person to work around your house. If your parents are well enough to get themselves over to your house (and particularly if they're fit enough to do it two or three times a week), they're well enough to help instead of hinder the work you have to do.

This is classical conditioning. You're telling your parents, "My house is not a place to goof off. It's not a resort, it's not the neighborhood bar or the Elks club. If you want to arrange a visit ahead of time, at a time that's convenient for me, I'll plan to do nothing but talk to you. But if you want to repeatedly barge in unannounced, you won't get coffee, you won't get my full attention, and you won't get a chance to sit down and get comfortable."

Naturally, do this warmly, with sincere apologies for being unavailable. But do it nonetheless.

9

Whose House Is This, Anyway?

OKAY, NOW THAT we've got your parents dialed into the fact that your house doesn't have unlimited visiting hours, and that you haven't had "Mom and Dad" embroidered on the pillow shams in the spare bedroom, let's talk about you.

Parents take a bad rap for abusing their visiting privileges, but what about you? Many of you act as if moving out of your parents' house was only a temporary relocation. You act as if you still live there. You drop by unannounced, you help yourself to what's in the refrigerator, and you use their attic and basement as your own personal U-Store-It. You insist on having everything, especially your bedroom, preserved just as it was when you were a full-time resident there.

Wrong, wrong, wrong.

I hate to be the bearer of bad tidings, but the day you established a separate permanent residence of your own, you were reduced to guest status in your parents' house. I know they tell you that "There will always be a place for you here" and that "This will always be your home," but those are expressions of affection, not an invitation to regard their *casa* as *su casa*.

Watch Your Language

First, let's define terms. Adults who say, "I'm going home for Christmas"—and mean they're spending the holidays at their parents' house—are seriously confused. Your parents' house is *their* house and *their* home. Presumably, you have one of your own—you know, the place you go back to every day after work, the place where you sleep, the place where your cat or dog or your spouse or children live?

Whether you live alone in a studio apartment or with your spouse and three kids in a four-bedroom ranch, *that*, not your parents' house, is home.

Referring to your parents' house as "home" is a pretty sorry reflection on your independence, and it's a blatant insult to the people you live with. Is your house or apartment just a temporary residence? Are your spouse and kids just a temporary family? Are you going back to your real family soon?

Where *you* live is home. Period. Get used to it. Start saying, "I'm going to my *folks' house* for Christmas" or "I'm spending Thanksgiving *with my parents.*" *Stop* saying, "I'm going home for the holidays."

My Old Childhood Home

At no time is the "My parents' house is my house" syndrome more evident than when your parents decide to get rid of the old homestead.

Mary, a thirty-one-year-old real estate agent, said, "When my father retired, my parents sold our family house, and all the furniture in it, and bought a houseboat in Florida. Honest to God—a houseboat. They didn't understand what that house meant to my brother and me. We grew up there. That was our home.

"What about Christmas? What about Thanksgiving? Those used to be big family holidays. Now we're supposed to cram ten people into that plywood garbage scow they live in? It's absurd."

Sorry, Mary. Your parents can do whatever they want to with *their* house. You have no more say in what they do with their house than they have in what you do with yours.

But That's My Childhood You're Talking About

Adult children want their parents to keep the home of their youth forever intact as a shrine to their childhood memories.

"We'd like to move to Florida," Mary wants to hear her parents say, "but that would mean Mary wouldn't be able to come home once or twice a year and play with the stuffed animals lined up on her bed. I guess we'd better stay here."

If you want to preserve the old family home that badly, why don't you buy it yourself if your parents put it on the market? *You* make the house payments. *You* pay the utilities. *You* take responsibility for maintaining it. (Wait a minute, do I hear you saying it's not *that* important? I didn't think so.)

And what about those of you who are offended when your parents box up your high school pennants and your faded Beach Boys posters, and turn *your* bedroom into a guest room? You're aghast: How could your parents dismantle this memorial to your youth, your glorious past?

Well, folks, the key word here is *past*. You had an eighteen-year lease on one bedroom and a bath in your parents' house, but the lease has expired.

The New Rules

Since your parents' house isn't your house anymore, isn't it time you stopped:

Dropping by unannounced? Do you call your parents before you stop over? Or do you just pop in whenever it suits you? Set the precedent of *always* calling before you drop by. Always ask, "Are you going to be home later this afternoon? I thought I'd stop by after I pick up the kids." Or, "I'd like to borrow Dad's drill. When would be a good time to come over?"

No matter how many times your parents say, "Any time is fine; you know that" or "You don't have to ask to come over here," do it anyway. Respond with "Oh, I know I don't need to ask, but I just wanted to make sure it was a convenient time for you."

This also delivers the message that you'd like *them* to do the same for *you.*

Letting yourself in with a key to their house? This is a violation of your parents' privacy. Having the kids grown and gone gives many couples a new feeling of freedom—which they can't enjoy if they never know when you're going to stroll through the front door. Would you like your parents to let themselves into *your* house at will?

Go through the formality of ringing the doorbell or knocking on the door, then wait for your parents to answer it. Give them their key back—or, if they insist on you keeping a key (in case of the inevitable emergency they know is right around the corner), put it in a drawer somewhere and stop carrying it on your key ring.

Acting as if you're still a kid when you're at your parents' house? Do you help yourself to whatever is in the refrigerator, leave your dirty dishes lying around, and bring your laundry over for your mother to do?

This isn't how you treat your friends when you visit (because if you did, you wouldn't have any friends), so don't subject your parents to this sort of behavior. Your parents' house is not the place to take your vacation, so don't expect free food, maid service, and the red-carpet treatment.

Remember: You can't treat your parents' house like it's your own house, and then get upset when they return the favor.

Staying with your parents for weeks on end? Do you moan and groan when your parents come to stay with you for two weeks, but then do the same to them? Once you've moved out, your parents set up a new routine, and regardless of what that new routine is, you disrupt it when you visit. When you stay with them, you do much more than just muss up the sheets in your old room. You use the bathrooms, the kitchen, the washer and dryer, and the TV. You eat their food, block their driveway, and stay up making noise long after they've gone to bed.

Short-term, that disruption is welcome. Long-term, it is just as much a pain to them as it is to you when the situation is reversed. Don't believe them when they say, "But you've only been here for a week; can't you stay another few days? Don't rush off, we love having you here." What else are they going to say—"Get the hell out of our house"?

Use the same rules for visiting your parents that you'd like to impose when they're visiting you. Make your visit a model of how visits between the two of you should be.

Moving Back in with Your Parents

If you are over twenty-two, or have been out of school for more than a year, you have no business living with your parents. If you haven't moved out yet, stop being a mooch and start packing. And don't move back in except for extraordinary circumstances—and I do mean extraordinary—like:

1. An illness so devastating that you are unable to care for yourself, and you have no spouse, child, or friend to take care of you.

2. A financial setback so staggering that you can't afford even a fleabag apartment to live in.

In every other situation, accept responsibility for your own room and board. *None* of the following, despite what you may tell yourself—or despite what your parents may tell you—are good reasons for imposing on your parents:

Rationalization #1: They have plenty of room. Adult children think parents with large houses won't mind someone staying in the spare bedroom for a while. But it's impossible to confine your activities to only the spare bedroom. You're living in their whole house.

Bear in mind that you're going to have your own spare bedroom one of these days. Do you want to hear your parents say, "You've got plenty of room" as they're loading their belongings into your house?

Mark, a twenty-eight-year-old soldier, decided that the army wasn't the life for him, and asked his parents if he could stay with them when he got out—just until he found an apartment, he said. Thirteen months later, he was still living with his parents, and complaining about them to anyone who would listen. "They treat me like a kid. They always want to know where I'm going and what I'm doing. Why can't they stay in their part of the house and let me stay in mine, and leave me alone?"

His part of the house? Is Mark making the mortgage payments on that part of the house? I don't think so.

Rationalization #2: They asked me to move in. No parent in the world is going to say, "I know you've lost your job and you're broke, but don't ask us for a place to stay. You can sleep in the city park." Parental responsibility forces your parents to remind you frequently that "There will always be room for you here"—no matter how they really feel about it.

So don't assume they mean it.

Rationalization #3: It's only temporary. If it's your friends you're moving in with, temporary is two or three weeks—a month, max. You wouldn't dream of moving in on your friends for a year. But with your parents, *temporary* often means *indefinitely.*

One couple (ages twenty-nine and thirty-five) moved in with the wife's parents until the husband could get a new job; he'd been laid off from his old one. Four months later he had a job, but they decided to stay until they could save up enough for a small down payment on a house. Ten months later, they're still saving and still living in Mom and Dad's house.

If you've been living with your parents for more than a month, you're way overdue to leave. Get your own place, and stop acting as if you're entitled to a free ride.

Rationalization #4: I can't let my kids live in a slum. If, conveniently, your parents happen to live in a nice house in a nice neighborhood, it may seem preferable to live with them than to move into a run-down apartment in a low-rent district if that's all you could afford. After all, you can't let your children live in less than the finest available style, can you? (Your parents may even be using that argument on you.)

Nancy, a thirty-nine-year-old secretary, got divorced and moved back to her hometown—and back in with her parents. As a secretary, she wasn't making much money, but she had good references, and was able to get an above-average secretarial salary. But she had no thoughts of moving out of her parents' house.

"I suppose I could afford a small two-bedroom apartment," she said. "But what kind of life is that for my nine-year-old daughter? She should be in a nice house with a yard and a dog. Besides, this way I can afford to buy her good clothes and toys."

So for Christmas, the nine-year-old got three hundred dollars' worth of clothes and toys, while Grandma and Grandpa footed the housing bill.

Someday Nancy may have a nice house of her own in a nice neighborhood. Would she want to have two frail old people living with her so they wouldn't have to move into a tiny two-bedroom apartment with no yard and no dog?

Fat chance.

THE GOLDEN RULE OF PARENTAL RELATIONS

The bottom line to all interaction with your parents— whether it's visiting them, moving back in with them, or taking them out to Dairy Queen for a hot fudge sundae— is the Golden Rule of Parental Relations:

Do unto your parents as you would have them do unto you. And keep doing it until they get the hint that they're supposed to do the same.

10

The First National Family Bank

WHEN IT COMES to money, your mother did a number on you. Oh, she didn't mean to, of course. Your dear old mother would never intentionally try to con you. (Would she?) It's just that your mother believes in a delightful, compelling, but totally nonexistent concept called *Family Money.*

Family Money is the idea that all the money Dad earns belongs not just to him, but to Mom and the kids as well. It is the idea that all the money and property your parents have amassed over the years is yours, too.

Your mother believes in Family Money with all her heart, and she has spent years convincing you that it exists. She tells you how hard she and your father have worked so that you'll have something when they are gone. Every time you see her, she gives you a list of their checking account numbers, savings account numbers, CD and IRA numbers, and the address and phone number of their bank, their accountant, and their attorney. Your brothers and sisters all have numerous copies of this information, and another copy is taped to the back of your father's desk, where burglars couldn't find it but where you could get it if "something happened" and the other 239 copies were lost.

Now Let's Hear from Dad

The catch is that Dad doesn't see it this way. Oh, he never contradicts Mom, publicly or privately, which is why she's been able to convince you and herself that the Family Money concept is real. However, as far as he's concerned, it's *his* money, *he* earned it, and *he'll* dole it out as *he* sees fit.

Dad has this strange idea that you're old enough to take care of yourself. He doesn't worry about how you're going to support yourself when he's gone—you seem to be doing that just fine while he's still alive. He doesn't want to give you a $100,000 inheritance so you won't ever have to worry about money again. As far as he's concerned, if there's something left over for you to inherit when he dies, that's great. If not... well, nobody ever gave him anything and he got by just fine. He assumes you will, too.

Family Money—But Whose Family?

This difference in attitude is most apparent if one of your parents dies.

If your father should die (heaven forbid), your mother may refuse to remarry in order to keep someone else (her new husband) from getting his hands on *your* money. Widowed mothers have even been known to cut back on their standard of living so they won't use up *your* inheritance.

If your mother does remarry, she will draw up an airtight will to make sure you get everything she and your father accumulated before his death. And even then, she will worry that her new husband and his children might try to take it away from you.

On the other hand, if your mother should die (heaven forbid), the Family Money concept goes up in smoke. Your father is suddenly managing *his* and *only his* money. He may decide to stockpile it for his old age, or he may decide to blow every last cent. He may take a world cruise. He may move to Florida and start up a flamingo farm. Or, worse, he may remarry.

When Dad remarries, the Family Money concept is reborn, except that this time the family is Dad and his new wife, not Dad and you. You're out of luck, because Dad considers his financial responsibility to be first to himself, second to his wife—whoever she may be—and third to his children, provided they still are children.

Grown children rarely make the list.

The Gimme Principle

So stop counting your parents' silverware, doing mental appraisals on their house, and asking if they've shopped around for the highest interest rates on their CDs. Don't have a talk with your parents, despite what the financial counselors tell you, about what estate planning they've done to make sure you get every possible nickel. (If your parents haven't taken care of that—or don't want to—your asking about it won't convince them to.)

If you do end up with an inheritance, wonderful. But it's important to remember that it's *their* money, and they can do whatever they want to do with it. You're not *entitled* to anything, because it's not your money. Whatever you get is a gift.

Naturally you're not going to be happy if your parents decide to leave their $3 million estate to St. Lefty's Home for Orphaned Penguins. But unless you can prove in court that they were stark, staring mad when they made out their will, you'll have to live with their decision.

Your "Fair Share"

Your parents' will is not the place to expect issues of jealousy, success, or sacrifice to be settled. You may feel that you "deserve" more than an equal share of your parents' estate because you're a waiter and your brother is a high-priced management consultant. Or you may think your parents "owe" you more because you've let your mother live with you for the past five years, while your sister hasn't chipped in a dime toward her support.

But don't expect your parents to even things out by dying and distributing their estate in the proportions you feel are appropriate. Most parents hand out an even split, regardless of your circumstances or past contributions to them. So instead of feeling that you should get the bulk of their estate, figure out a way to make it right *today,* while they're still alive. Devote more time to your own career, if your brother's success bothers you so much. Start charging your mother room and board, if you feel that she's freeloading. Or send your deadbeat sister a bill for *her* fair share of Mom's expenses.

Money as a Weapon

Giving up the "my fair share" concept also stops your parents from using your inheritance as a weapon to keep you under their thumbs: "If you marry that loser, I'll cut you out of my will" or "If you don't straighten up, I'll leave everything to your brother" or "My next-door neighbor is nicer to me than you are; I may leave everything to her." Sometimes it's not a direct threat; it's just a vague suggestion that the money goes to those who are in favor. And staying in favor means doing it their way.

In less polite circles, it's called blackmail.

If your parents' estate is substantial, you may find your-

self bowing to this sort of pressure. The older they get—
and the closer to death—the more you may try to
ingratiate yourself with them. You think, "They won't live
that much longer. I can be nice to them for a few more
years."

And maybe you can. But parents (especially nasty ones)
have a way of living much longer than you ever thought
possible.

Would you still knuckle under if you knew they were
going to live to be ninety-five? Would you still knuckle
under if you knew that by the time they died, their estate
would be gone, eaten up by medical bills? And can you
afford to knuckle under knowing that they could change
their will at the last minute?

Remember that unless you've seen your parents' will,
you don't really know what they're going to do with their
money. And even if you have seen it, they can run down to
their attorney's office tomorrow morning and have a new
one drawn up—and you'd never know it.

Stop the Threats

Parents threaten you with the loss of your inheritance in
order to control you. The only antidote is to exhibit total
indifference toward their money.

> **YOUR PARENTS:** I ought to cut you out of my will.
>
> **YOU:** It's your money. Do whatever you want with it.
>
> **YOUR PARENTS:** I'm serious. As little as you come to see me
> or call me, I ought to leave everything to the church.
>
> **YOU:** It's your money, and it's your decision what to do with it.
>
> **YOUR PARENTS:** You'll be sorry when you can't get your
> hands on this house.
>
> **YOU:** Surely you don't think I want you to die so I can have
> your house, do you?

YOUR PARENTS: Maybe I'll just leave everything to your sister.

YOU: It's your money..., etc., etc.

Your parents won't use a threat that doesn't bother you. Maintain the "It's your money" line, and they'll stop beating you over the head with it.

For the "I'll-leave-everything-to-your-sister" parents, who threaten to leave their cash to whichever child treats them best, use an end-run strategy. Schedule a meeting with your brothers and sisters—who are probably also being threatened with no dough—and agree to split your parents' estate equally, regardless of how your parents divide up the loot in their will. (If your brothers or sisters are less than trustworthy, you might consider getting this agreement in writing.)

Then, when your parents threaten to cut you out of their will, you can say, "Arnold, Francine, and I had a little talk about these threats, and we've agreed that whatever you leave us we will split an even three ways."

However, if you think this might push your parents into a St. Lefty's donation, just keep quiet and be content with the knowledge that their threats are empty ones.

Mother, Can You Spare a Dime?

The idea that your parents are simply holding all this money for you until they die may make you impatient to get your hands on it now. You may think your parents ought to be generous with gifts and loans—sort of an advance against your inheritance. Haven't they always told you that if you ever needed money, all you had to do was ask?

What you've failed to notice is that they're no longer serious about that little suggestion. They got *un*serious right after you landed your first good-paying job.

When kids first go out on their own, "borrowing" money from parents is common. In fact, parents often initiate the loan and make the repayment terms vague: "You can pay us back when you get squared away and are making more money."

These loans are more like gifts. They're made at a very low interest rate, and repayment is often canceled as a graduation or wedding present.

But that's kid's stuff. You have no business, now that you're older and squared away, hounding your parents for low-interest loans with long-term payment plans that stretch away into eternity.

Your parents have gotten older, too, and they aren't nearly as enthused about coughing up the money as they once were. While you're standing there with your hand out, they're worried about living on a fixed income during their retirement years.

You wouldn't say to a close friend, "Lend me four thousand dollars at 3 percent interest, and I'll pay you back sometime over the next five or ten years." Your friend would laugh in your face.

But some of you think your parents should cash in their certificates of deposit, take a 10 percent interest penalty, and make that money available to you. In fact, you're insulted if they don't.

You don't *expect* your friends to lend you money. And you certainly wouldn't expect them to take a loss.

So why do you expect your parents to?

Be Adult About Borrowing Money

If you nevertheless must borrow money from your parents, follow these guidelines:

Be realistic about your parents' resources. Don't assume that your parents *have* money to lend you. Just because they appear to be loaded doesn't mean they are. To you,

$150,000 in the bank is quite a stash. To your parents, who may have to make it last for twenty-five or thirty more years, it doesn't look like such a fortune.

Take rejection gracefully. If you ask for a loan, and your parents can't or won't give it to you, have the good grace to say, "Thanks anyway," and never mention it again.

Don't say, "You're kidding. Why not?" Don't beg. And don't try to make them feel guilty—now or later—with comments like "If only you'd loaned me that money three years ago, I know I'd have a whole chain of trampoline dealerships by now."

Be fair. If you do get the loan, give your parents no less than the same interest rate they could get at a good-quality bank. And I don't mean passbook rates. I mean the rate they could get on a CD for the same amount of money over the same time period you want the loan for.

Be nice. Remember that these are people who have a soft spot for you. Don't take advantage of them.

Be generous, instead of expecting generosity. Be really adult about it, and give them a *higher* interest rate than they could get on a CD. Split the difference between the best rate you could get on a loan and the best rate they could get on a CD. For example, if a car loan would cost you 13 percent at a bank, and your parents could earn 7 percent with a CD, offer to pay them 10 percent.

"You'd make more by lending it to me than leaving it in the bank" is a great pitch to give your parents. It makes you look mature and responsible and all that.

One man said he made this offer to his mother a few years ago, and now she calls him every six months and wants to know if he'd like to borrow a few thousand dollars. With the current low interest rates, her son looks like a good way to make money.

Make sure your parents understand what they're getting into. Tell them exactly how much you want to borrow, how much interest you will pay, how long you want to borrow the money for, and what your monthly payments will be.

(You can get a loan amortization schedule at a bank or library.) There should be no surprises.

And remind your parents that this is no savings account. They can't call in their note if they need the money unexpectedly, which, by the way, is another good reason for giving them a higher interest rate than they can get from a bank. A bank will give them their principal back on demand. You won't.

Put it in writing. No handshake deals, no unclear payment dates, no vague promises. Go to an office supply store and buy a promissory note form (they cost less than a dollar). Fill out the form as carefully as you would if you were *lending* the money instead of borrowing it. Then sign it, have it notarized, make a copy for yourself, and give your parents the original.

Ignore any protests from your parents that you don't need to do this. You do need to do this.

And don't be surprised if there aren't any protests. "My parents' reaction to all this formal stuff," one woman said, "was delight. They said, 'Thanks,' and were all smiles as they locked the promissory note away in their safe." She paused thoughtfully. "Does that mean they don't trust me?"

No, it means they're glad you take seriously the responsibility of owing them money. They're happy to know you intend to pay them back.

Make it a two-way street. In the rare, but not totally unheard-of, instance where your parents want to borrow money from *you,* make the loan just as businesslike as when you're the borrower. Do this for two reasons: (1) It will make your parents feel less like they're taking charity from their kids, and (2) you may need that piece of paper to get money out of their estate if they die.

It's never too late to repay a loan. If you've already borrowed money from your parents and have defaulted or have fallen behind on your payments, it's not too late to make amends. Start paying them back, even if it's only ten or twenty dollars a month.

It's the adult thing to do.

The Gimme Principle Revisited

Under the new "I'll act like an adult, and you treat me like one" program, you also have to stop expecting to be inundated with gifts and/or money for Christmas, your birthday, your wedding (especially if it's not your first), your new job, or the birth of your next child.

Years ago, the question "What do you want for Christmas?" prompted you to write a thirty-seven-page list of toys, clothes, vehicles, and merchandise, including brand names, model numbers, and the stores that carried those items. Today the only correct response is "You don't need to buy me anything. We'll all be together; that's what really counts."

And you should mean it.

Maybe You Expect Too Much

Of course, it's no fun when your parents take you seriously. The first time you get a little birthday card that says, "We'll take you out to dinner the next time you're here," instead of the two dozen presents you're used to, it's a big letdown. It means your childhood is over. Your parents have started treating you like an adult.

Shucks.

But if your reaction is that your parents are just being stingy, think again. You may be:

1. Confusing money with love.
2. Still buying into the Family Money theory (as in "It's my money, too, so why don't they spend some of it on me?").

3. Forgetting that only children expect to make a haul on holidays.

Beware of Parents Bearing Gifts

Besides, gifts, especially major ones, may come back to
haunt you.

Kathy, who lives only three miles from her parents, told
this story:

> "My parents bought me a beautiful new Buick Regal for a
> graduation present eight years ago. But for eight years my
> father has acted as if *he* owns it. If it's dirty, he says, 'We didn't
> buy you that car so you could turn it into a pigpen.' If I don't
> change the oil regularly, he says, 'We didn't buy you that car so
> you could ruin the engine.' If he drives by and the car isn't in
> the garage, he says, 'We didn't buy you that car so you could
> leave it out in the sun to fade the paint.'
>
> "If I could afford it," Kathy said with frustration, "I'd buy a
> new car and give him this one back, so he'd stop bugging me."

Some parents use the "You pick it out; I'll pay for it"
technique:

> Gena's parents offered to buy her a couch as a housewarm-
> ing present. Anything up to a thousand dollars, they said. Nat-
> urally, with that much money involved, her mother wanted to
> help shop for it. But everything Gena picked out, her mother
> vetoed: "No, I don't think that color would be right with your
> carpeting." "No, all those loose pillows will drive you crazy."
> "No, that fabric doesn't wear well."
>
> It was six grueling weeks before Gena found a couch her
> mother would approve for purchase—and even then, it wasn't
> the couch Gena really wanted.

And when the presents get bigger, the problems get bigger:

Dan's parents had a two-acre lot in the mountains that they had planned to build a retirement home on. But when Dan announced he was getting married, they changed their minds, and decided to make the lot a wedding present to their son.

Dan and his new wife Karen were thrilled, and they built a house on the property. But the thrill began to wear off as months dragged by and Dan's parents couldn't find the time to execute a quit claim deed making the property legally Dan and Karen's. After three years, Dan's parents still refer to the house and land as "ours," and Dan's father frequently shows up unannounced to work on "our" property: planting new trees, cutting down dead ones, mulching the lawn—things he says he knows the "kids" don't have time to do.

So buy your own major presents, and let your parents keep their hard-earned money. Everybody will be happier.

Tightwad Parents

My parents are so tight, you may be thinking, that getting expensive presents hardly ranks as one of my big concerns. "Tight is an understatement," one son said. "My wife and I spend three hundred dollars in gas and lodging to go see my parents, and when we get there, they think *we* should take *them* out to dinner."

Here are a few thoughts on life with cheap parents:

Remember 1929? Parents raised in the Depression, or in its aftermath, have a gut-level terror of being poor. Nothing will ever convince them that it won't happen again. For them, the only safe bet is to prepare for the worst, hope for the best, and hang on to every cent they've got.

A penny saved is a penny earned. Parents who want to save a few dollars by buying $1.99 bath towels for their newly remodeled $8,000 bathroom should be allowed to do so without comment. Everybody has his or her own idea of what being thrifty means.

You're rich, aren't you? Some parents regard *you* as having a fortune. You've gone out of your way to convince them that you're a success, and they believe you. That's why, with a perfectly clear conscience, they can let you fly your spouse and three kids from Cheyenne, Wyoming, to Fort Lauderdale to see them, then expect you to wine and dine them.

Back to your friends again. If you want more from your parents in the way of money or gifts than you would expect from your friends, you are expecting too much. Your parents have spent plenty of money on you in the past twenty or thirty or forty years. Get off the dole.

11

Whose Love Life Is This, Anyway?

FEW TOPICS generate stronger emotions, bigger fights, or longer-lasting problems with your parents than your love life. Most parents think that whom you date, live with, or marry is 100 percent their business, and they will encourage, pester, or try to coerce you into doing what *they* think is best. If you're dating a doctor, they're delighted. They will take out a second mortgage on their house, if necessary, to finance your wedding. But if your intended has been unemployed for the past three years, well...

That's the Best You Could Do?

Whether you and the object of your affection are celebrating your fifteenth wedding anniversary or going out on your first date, almost all parents think you could have done better. Every mother knows that there isn't a woman alive who's good enough for her son, and every father is convinced that no man is worthy of his daughter.

- "When we go to see my mother-in-law," one man said, "she kisses me hello as if I had thirty-seven different communicable diseases."

- "My father never lets an opportunity go by," a very successful woman said, "to mention that I make more money than my husband does."

- "All I hear from my father," another woman said, "is 'I can't believe you're going out with that drip.'"

In determining whether you've made the proper choice, few parents ask the key question: "Are you two really in love?" Sure, love helps, but your parents are more concerned about the truly important factors like social standing, size of paycheck, housekeeping ability, breeding, and racial, religious, and age compatibility.

Your parents want to make sure you're not only getting someone good enough for you, but someone good enough for *them*. And they want to make sure that this interloper won't "take you away," alienate your affections, or in any way usurp their position as the center of your universe.

But despite what your parents think, *your love life is none of their business.*

Now, how do we convince *them* of that?

Do Your Parents Have Any Rights?

Okay, your parents are family. They get to have an opinion. And we'll even let them give you that opinion, provided they do so in a friendly, constructive way. If they feel strongly about it, they are allowed to say, "I can't stand that twerp—don't bring him (or her) around here again." (You should make sure, of course, that they understand that *you* might decide to not come around again either.)

But that's all they are entitled to.

They are not entitled to threaten you, bully you, harass you, criticize you, make you miserable, or in any way try to split you and your partner up.

So if your parents are giving you a hard time, make a stand here and now. Tell them:

> "I won't listen to one more snide remark or one more word of criticism about my marriage [or my date or my living arrangements]—which means that either you stop making those remarks or I stop coming over here."

And that also applies to parents who think they're being subtle about their dislike.

> "My wife, Lynette, is older than I am, has been divorced, and has a four-year-old daughter," one man said. "My parents are appalled that I married someone who had already 'been around the block,' to use their term. They are superficially polite, but they are always making little digs. My mother keeps asking Heather (the four-year-old) if she's seen her daddy lately and calling her 'poor baby.' My dad just ignores her because she's not *his* granddaughter.
>
> "If I say anything to my folks, they say, 'We like Lynette just fine, and Heather is a little doll. There's no problem.'
>
> "There's no problem except that these visits put everybody on edge, and afterwards, Lynette and I always end up in a fight."

Most of you were raised on too much Perry Mason. You think that unless you can *prove* a remark is derogatory, you shouldn't say anything about it. But this isn't a court of law, and you're not trying someone for murder. This is everyday life, and the only evidence you need that a comment was intended as a slight is that unpleasant, annoyed feeling you get.

Put Your Cards on the Table

Don't accept your parents' evasions, like "We like Lynette just fine" or "There's no problem." Point out exactly what they're doing that bothers you:

"Mom, every time we come over, you make a point of mentioning Heather's father, and saying how sorry you feel for her because her parents are divorced. While I'm sure you do feel that way, this constant focus on Lynette's divorce makes both Lynette and me uncomfortable. I know you're unhappy about my marrying a divorced woman who has a child, but I want you to stop mentioning it."

Don't get into a discussion of why they don't like your spouse, because their reasons won't be anything you can change (he doesn't make enough money, she is too old for you, or you don't pay as much attention to your parents as you used to).

Just tell them that you know what they're doing and you want them to stop.

Watch What You Say

If your mother and father actually like your spouse, don't jeopardize this precarious relationship by sharing your marital problems with your parents. You're their little darling, and anybody who doesn't treat you right is automatically and often permanently on their hate list.

So be careful what you tell them.

"My husband and I had a big fight about six months ago," Sally said. "He stormed out and didn't come home until three in the morning. I made the mistake of telling my mother about it the next day, and of course she wanted me to go straight downtown to the courthouse and file for divorce.

"I hardly remember now what Don and I were fighting about, but my mother remembers every little detail. She's been very cool to Don since then, and she keeps asking me if I'm sure I want to stay with a man who is so mean to me."

Of course, even more annoying are parents who don't think *you* are such a great catch, so they side with your spouse:

"Well, Sally, if you didn't nag Don so much, he wouldn't get so mad. You're always picking at him, and I don't think that's right. I would never talk to your father like that."

Thanks a million for the support, Mom.

It's better to just leave your parents out of it, because they can't be objective, and they can't forget what you tell them.

'TIL DEATH (OR OUR PARENTS) DO US PART

The high point of your parents' involvement in your love life is, of course, your wedding. Parents go to one extreme or the other.

> "That's wonderful! We were beginning to think you'd never get married (or married again)."

> or

> "Are you sure you should be doing this? You two haven't been dating very long." (If they don't like your fiancé, "haven't been dating very long" means anything under ten years.)

Either way it goes, I can guarantee that by the time the ceremony actually takes place, you and your parents will barely be speaking to each other. That's because everybody thinks they own the wedding.

- You think you are in charge of the wedding because you're the one who is getting married.
- The bride's parents think they're in charge of the wedding because they are usually the ones paying for it.
- Whichever set of parents is giving the most extravagant wedding present thinks they get to be at least partly in charge.

Never forget that dollars equal votes, and anyone who contributes so much as five dollars to your wedding will want a say in the plans. Weddings by committee are no fun, and if your mother and your future mother-in-law have an equal vote, the results could be disastrous.

Since Miss Manners, Dear Abby, and Ann Landers deal almost daily with wedding problems, I'll be brief.

What Size Wedding?

When thinking about what size wedding you want, bear in mind this theorem: The problems generated by any wedding will be exactly one size larger than the wedding itself. A small wedding will generate medium-size problems. A medium-size wedding will generate large problems. A large wedding will cause astronomical problems.

A corollary to this theorem: Elopements will generate *years* of bitter complaints from both sides of the family.

Before asking your parents' advice, remember that parents like big weddings. They like the pomp and ceremony and they like to settle up old debts: "You have to have a big wedding. We've been buying wedding presents for all our friends' kids for years. Now it's our turn to collect."

Who's Going to Pay for It?

In the old days, the bride's parents always paid for the wedding (unless the groom's parents were very wealthy and the bride's parents were very poor). Today, you have to factor in a few other considerations.

Your age. If one or both of you is over thirty, pay for the wedding yourselves, even if it reduces the size of the wedding you originally wanted.

(A note to older grooms: If you don't pay for the wedding, her parents will think you're a wimp, a cheapskate, and a financial failure who can't afford to get married. Not a good way to start off relations with the new in-laws.)

If you are between twenty-five and thirty, it depends on your financial circumstances, your parents' financial circumstances, and how your parents react when you say, "We're only having a small wedding, because that's all we can afford." If they say, "That's sensible, dear," you're on your own. But if they say, "Our daughter have a small wedding? We won't hear of it," call the caterer.

If you are under twenty-five, you can reasonably expect your parents to underwrite some or all of the wedding. But adjust your wedding to fit their financial situation. Don't be like the twenty-four-year-old daughter who said, "My parents got divorced, and I realize money's tight for both of them right now, but they always promised me a big wedding. I don't think I should be cheated out of it just because *their* marriage fell apart."

Ask your parents for a budget if they offer to pay for your wedding. *Then don't go over it by so much as one dollar.*

Contributions from both parents. The groom, if he's under twenty-five, can also say to his parents, "We're only having a small wedding, because that's all we can afford," and see if they want to chip in. But don't pit the bride's parents against the groom's parents to see who can contribute the most money.

And don't do this at all if the bride's father might take it as an insult to his ability to pay for his daughter's wedding.

Your previous marriages. If this is a second marriage for only one of you, your parents might pay for the wedding if you're young and poor.

But if this is a second marriage for both parties, pay for your own wedding. How many trips down the aisle do you expect your parents to finance?

Your financial situation. Regardless of your age, if you and your fiancé's combined income approaches or exceeds your parents', pay for your own wedding.

Establish the Rules

With luck, this will be the last wedding you have—so, as the Burger King commercial suggests, "Have it your way." Don't let all your relatives harass you into a wedding you don't want.

The best way to do that is to tell everybody right from the start what's what. Take a lesson from a woman who failed to do that:

> Janine decided early on that she wanted no children in her wedding: no little ring bearers having to go to the bathroom in the middle of the ceremony, no tiny flower girls stopping to talk to their mommies halfway down the aisle.
>
> So she was understandably upset when her future mother-in-law announced that she'd asked her best friend's granddaughter to be in the wedding. But Janine was afraid to say anything for fear of upsetting her new family.
>
> Her fiancé said, "I'm sure that if you'd told Mom ahead of time that you didn't want children in the wedding, she never would have set that up. She was just trying to be helpful."

That's debatable, but that's also the excuse everyone gives for meddling in your wedding. Be firm, or they'll take it away from you.

> Ted and Adrianne, both divorced, decided on a quick city-hall ceremony with no family, just their respective best friends as witnesses, followed by a weekend in Palm Springs. They visited Adrianne's parents, some three states away, and announced they were getting married. But before they could explain what they had in mind, Adrianne's father said, "You name the time and the place, and we'll be there. We don't care how small the wedding is or where in the world you have it, but we wouldn't dream of missing it."
>
> Ted and Adrianne ended up with not only their best friends there, but their four parents, three brothers and sisters, and one grandparent—all of whom were from out of town and

needed lodging, meals, and transportation. The parents insisted on throwing a dinner for everyone. The grandparent insisted that the wedding be held in a church instead of city hall. The best friends felt obligated to buy wedding presents (even though Ted and Adrianne had told them not to), because Ted's sister started a gift list to make sure there'd be no duplications.

By the time it was over, Ted and Adrianne wished they'd gone to Las Vegas and gotten married in a pink plastic chapel on the Strip.

AS IF ONE SET OF PARENTS WEREN'T ENOUGH

I hereby move that the following terms be abolished from the English language, that they be added to the Bureau of Television Standard's list of words you can't say on television, and that anyone using them be subjected to a ten-thousand-dollar fine, ten years in prison, or both:

1. Daughter-in-law
2. Son-in-law
3. Mother-in-law
4. Father-in-law

These terms should be replaced immediately and permanently with terms like *my husband's father* or *my wife's mother.*

I also move that the saying "You're not losing a son; you're gaining a daughter" (or vice versa) be discontinued, since it was never true in the first place.

And finally, I recommend that anyone entering into marriage who considers calling his or her spouse's parents "Mom" and "Dad" should have the marriage postponed until such time as a thorough psychiatric examination can be performed.

Keeping Your Parent Quota to Two

You've already got two parents who drive you crazy; you don't need two more. It's hard enough to be the dutiful son or daughter to your own parents, without trying to be a dutiful son or daughter to people you hardly know. If you call your spouse's parents "Mom" and "Dad," you're giving them a license to treat you like a kid. So here are some tips on how to fend off the addition of two more parents to your life:

Take the initiative in getting on a first-name basis. As soon as you start spending any amount of time with the parents of your spouse, fiancé, or casual date, ask, "Do you mind if I call you Ralph and Irma?"—or whatever their names are. Don't wait for them to suggest what you should call them, because if they prefer "Mom" and "Dad," you're stuck.

Gradually move to a first-name basis, if you're already in the "Mom" and "Dad" trap and want to get out. At least once during your next visit, call each of them by his or her first name. Step that up to two or three times on the following visit, and keep escalating it until "Mom" and "Dad" have faded from your vocabulary.

If they question you on it, you can say—probably in all honesty—that you feel awkward calling someone other than *your* parents "Mom" and "Dad."

Discourage them from calling you and your spouse "the kids." Jokingly respond, "Boy, that's all you need is another kid, right?" Or "That's the nicest thing anybody's said to me all day—I wish I really were still young enough to be called a kid!"

Treat them as people, not parents. Don't act like a kid around them, don't accept favors you wouldn't accept from any other person their age, and discourage your spouse from reverting to childish behavior around them.

And remember: All the advice in this book works just as well with your spouse's parents as it does with your own.

YOUR PARENTS' LOVE LIFE

Just as your love life is none of your parents' business, their romantic involvements are none of your concern. Refrain from injecting yourself into the following situations:

Your parents' marriage. Your parents' marital problems are *their* problems, not yours. While you may want to lend a sympathetic ear, be wary of parents who want allies, not sympathy. Your best bet is to stay neutral and stay out of it.

Your parents' divorce. Before you choose up sides, remember that divorces are never 100 percent one person's fault—no matter how they look on the surface. Resist being drawn into this mess—you don't know what the whole story is.

Your parent's remarriage. You don't have to like the fact that one of your parents remarries after being divorced or widowed. You're entitled to your opinion. And you may want to voice that opinion if you think the new spouse has less-than-honorable intentions, such as being after your parent's money. But other than that, keep your opinions to yourself, even if you're:

1. Upset because your father marries a woman who's five years younger than you are.
2. Embarrassed because your sixty-seven-year-old mother is having a torrid love affair with a seventy-five-year-old man.
3. Angry because your widowed mother or father remarries before what you consider to be a "proper" mourning period has passed.

Older people get lonely, fall in love, desire sex, and want to get married—just like younger people. Be happy that *they* are happy and don't try to spoil it for them.

12

Whose Children Are These, Anyway?

YOUR PARENTS drive you crazy, and your children drive you crazy, but have you noticed that they never drive *each other* crazy? That's because they have so much in common.

1. Both of them want your undivided attention and total adoration—and both are mad when they don't get it.
2. Both of them think you should treat them better.
3. Both of them get a kick out of breaking your rules.
4. Both of them would rather be with each other than be with you.

They also have in common the fact that neither one of them does anything the way you think they should—especially your parents. Your parents are either Spoilers, who can't do enough for your children, or they're Ungrandparents, who have little or no interest in your kids.

THE SPOILER

"Look at All the Toys, Clothes, Candy, Movie Tickets, and Money that Grandma and Grandpa Have for You."

You name it, the Spoilers will do it for your children:

- Matt's grandmother fixes him whatever he wants for dinner —regardless of what she's made for everybody else. And if he changes his mind at the last minute, she'll make him something different.

- When Sean's grandparents baby-sit, they let him stay up as late as he wants to watch TV—even on school nights— because he's always "such a good boy" when he's at their house.

- Krista's grandfather takes her out to dinner once a month, and before each dinner he takes her shopping and buys her a new dress to wear for the occasion.

"Funny," you may be saying, "but I don't remember my parents treating *me* this well." So how come they treat your children like visiting royalty? It can be explained by these three simple principles:

Principle #1: For the grandparent, there are no consequences. Your parents heap huge amounts of love and money—and zero amounts of discipline—on your small children and are rewarded with increasing levels of affection and glee. Then they get to drop the kids off at your front door and go back to their quiet, child-free home.

You're the one who gets stuck listening to "I have a stomachache 'cause I ate four and a half pounds of cotton candy" or "Grandma picks up my toys for me; why won't you?" or "Grandpa doesn't make me go to bed at eight-thirty."

Principle #2: Grandparents are not responsible for how their grandchildren turn out. With you, your parents were on the hook for your eventual success or failure as a human being. With their grandchildren, that dirty job belongs to somebody else: you. Your parents can spoil your children unmercifully without worrying what it might do to the kids' little psyches. Their little psyches are *your* responsibility.

Principle #3: Grandparenting is a part-time job. Children wear best in small doses. Long before the kids get on their nerves, your parents can escape.

Are Spoilers Really All That Bad?

Before you get too hard on your parents, think back to what your grandparents used to do for you. Grandma used to let you eat all the chocolate chip cookies you wanted, and Grandpa used to take you to the neighborhood bar with him. But was it really that detrimental? Did it warp you for life? Not hardly.

Spoiling, in reasonable quantities from a loving source, doesn't spoil (as in "ruin") anybody.

The only time grandparent-grandchild relations become a problem is when:

Your children expect the same treatment from you that they get from their grandparents. This expectation can usually be nipped in the bud by telling the child that if he wants to see Grandma and Grandpa again, he'd better act like a normal human being when he's at home. Grandma's house is Vacationland, and he doesn't get to go to Vacationland unless (1) he's earned it, and (2) he recognizes the difference between Vacationland and real life.

You have the power to control how your children act. Don't blame your parents if your kids don't behave.

Your parents criticize you or your spouse to your children. The first time (or the next time) your children come home and say something like, "Grandma says she doesn't think Daddy is very nice to you," call your mother—out of earshot of your children, of course—and read her the riot act. Don't ask her nicely to please not make derogatory comments about your husband and your children's father. Don't try to reason with her or minimize the problem. Tell her (or your dad, if he's the culprit):

> "You are entitled to your opinion about my marriage; however, you are not entitled to discuss it with *my* children. The kids love you dearly and would be heartbroken if they couldn't see you. I hope you won't push it to that."

Your parents endanger your children's health or safety. If your father thinks tickling your children until they wet their pants is funny, or your mother thinks the baby's car seat is too much trouble to use, you have the right (and the obligation) to demand that they change their behavior.

Despite what your parents think, you are the final authority on your children. Grandparents who don't respect that authority should be told that you will cut off their visits or let them see their grandchildren only in your presence.

But don't overreact. You don't need to step in unless your parents really are acting irresponsibly. Remember that these two people have already raised at least one child (you) to adulthood without a major catastrophe. Six movies in two days will not make your child nearsighted, and a couple of sips of beer will not turn your child into an alcoholic—no matter how much you disapprove. The simple message, "Don't tell your Mom or Dad about this," which all grandparents deliver, clues the child in that what they're doing isn't all that smart.

By all means, encourage your children to spill the beans about any "Don't tell your Mom and Dad" activities, but again, don't act on them unless they're truly harmful. If you throw a fit about an overload of cotton candy, your children will never again tell you what they're up to, major or minor, with Grandma and Grandpa.

"Hand Over Those Kids"

The concept of presenting your parents with the next generation—as in "She presented her parents with a beautiful little grandson"—leads some parents to erroneously think they are part-owners of these new little beings.

Teachers, yes. Spoilers, yes. Surrogate parents? No.

Make it very clear that your children have only one set of parents. Set limits on visitations, gifts, and activities, and stick to them. If your parents abuse their privileges, cut them off or throw them out. And start early.

> A week before Kay was due to have her baby, there was a knock on her front door.
>
> "Surprise!" her mother said, carrying her three suitcases into the living room. "I knew you'd need help, with the baby about to arrive—so here I am!"
>
> Kay and her husband were appalled. And they were even more appalled when Mom stayed for another six weeks. But neither one of them had the nerve to tell Mom that she was grossly overstepping the boundaries of family togetherness.

Grandma's Day-Care Center

It is easy to take advantage of Spoilers—particularly when it comes to baby-sitting. Your mother is not running a day-care center, a foster home, or a call-any-time baby-sitting service. She and your father—regardless of what they say—do not want to baby-sit your kids for hours or days on end. They don't want you dropping off the kids at their place of work, and they don't want you to assume that there is no limit to their desire to take care of your children.

Your parents, however, will never tell you this. Where

their grandchildren are concerned, most grandmothers are incapable of saying no. They will claim to their dying breath that they can't get enough of those cute little rug rats, so bring them on over. But it's often not true, so follow these guidelines:

1. Count how many times your parents ask to see your children. I don't mean an indefinite "We'd love to see the kids." I mean a specific request to have them for the day, the afternoon, or the evening. Your belief that your parents want to see their grandchildren eight times a week might be off by as much as seven or eight.

2. Don't ask your mother to baby-sit every day while you work. If she wanted a full-time job, she'd already have one —and it probably wouldn't be baby-sitting.

3. Don't ask your parents to baby-sit more than two evenings a month. If you can't afford a baby-sitter, don't go out.

4. Don't ask your parents to do more than you'd ask a friend to do. If they want to do more, they'll volunteer.

5. For some grandparents, the joy of grandchildren wears off with time. An infant they couldn't get enough of grows into a seven-year-old they don't want to see more than once a month.

6. The older your parents are, the less you should ask them to baby-sit. They don't have the stamina.

7. Your children are *your* responsibility. Don't try to pawn them off on your parents.

THE UNGRANDPARENT

"Once Was Enough for Us, Thank You."

"My grandchildren are the darlingest little things in the world," a grandmother said, "but after five kids of my own, I don't want to change another diaper again as long as I live."

"Not having kids around the house," her husband

added, "is a relief. No screaming, no crying, no 'Take me here, take me there.' We did our child-raising bit. We're through."

Given the pleasure and benefits that children gain from a good relationship with their grandparents, this attitude is sad. Encourage your parents to spend time with your kids, but if they won't, there's not much you can do about it.

Just make sure that you haven't overburdened your parents with baby-sitting and child-raising responsibilities to the point that they are burned out on seeing your kids. And make sure *your* relationship with your parents—if it's not a good one—isn't what's standing in their way.

What's Best for the Kids?

Your children come first. They come before your parents' feelings, they come before your pride, and they come before your relationship with your parents.

If you can't stand your parents, but your kids adore them, let them all spend as much time together as possible. Grandparents and grandchildren are good for each other.

And just as you don't want your parents bad-mouthing you, watch what you say about *them* around your children. That's their grandparents you're talking about.

WHEN THERE AREN'T ANY KIDS TO FIGHT OVER

Having children can create problems with your parents, but the decision *not* to have children usually causes a furor. You hear:

- "How can you be so selfish? We have a right to have grand-children."

- "There must be something wrong with your marriage, if you're not having children."
- "You'll be sorry when you're old, and there's no one to take care of you."

We're talking about your parents' immortality here (or at least that's what they think). We're talking about passing their genes down through the generations. We're talking about *having children,* for heaven's sake, which in their day was a given.

And for some parents—the future Spoilers—we're talking about robbing them of the grandparenting experience they've been looking forward to.

So do them the courtesy of listening to what they have to say. Talk with them about it. Explain your reasons, and try to get them to see your point of view.

But once you've gone around a few times on this topic, your obligation to soothe their feelings ceases. You don't have to bow to parental pressure or be brow-beaten for deciding not to increase the world population. If necessary, get firm:

> "We've made our decision: We're not going to have children. From now on, I think it would be best if that subject were off limits."

13

The Great American Holiday Tradition

IT'S TAKEN WEEKS of careful shopping, gift wrapping, and car maintenance, but you're finally ready. You roll up your sleeves, take a deep breath, and get ready to start this year's running of The Annual Season's Greetings 500-Mile Road Rally. It's a grueling test of endurance—with the timing figured down to the split second—that goes something like this:

Christmas Eve

Noon: After a frantic morning of last-minute preparation, you make lunch for the family, load up the car with the kids and exactly half the presents, and drive to your in-laws' house, which is two hours west of yours. It's been hectic, but everyone's in a good mood, and during the drive the family sings all their favorite Christmas carols.

2:00 P.M.: You arrive at your in-laws' house, unload the kids and the presents, and spend all afternoon helping your mother-in-law fix an enormous Christmas Eve dinner of turkey, ham, mashed potatoes, gravy, dressing, rolls, and mincemeat pie. You're getting tired, but you still have enough energy to be cheerful to the bizarre collection of cousins, aunts, uncles, and other undefined relatives that parades in and out of the house.

5:00 P.M.: Prodded by your mother-in-law—"That's not all you're going to eat, is it?"—you stuff yourself.

7:00 P.M.: You help your fastidious mother-in-law clean up the kitchen, including washing the undersides of the windowsills and vacuuming behind the stove. You're wearing down fast.

8:00 P.M.: Everybody opens presents by the Christmas tree. Your father-in-law puts Christmas records on and plays them so loud that even the kids' shrieking doesn't drown out the music. Your mother-in-law mentions every fifteen minutes that it's a shame all of you can't spend the whole Christmas holiday together, but she supposes that (sigh) Christmas Eve is better than nothing.

11:00 P.M.: You reload the kids and the opened presents into the car and drive two hours back to your house. Your head keeps nodding dangerously close to the steering wheel, and your spouse keeps saying, "Are you sure you can drive?" "Yeah, yeah," you say, "I'm fine."

1:00 A.M.: You groggily unload the kids and the opened presents. The kids complain that they are too tired to get out of the car and want to sleep there for the night. You don't let them.

Christmas Day

6:00 A.M.: You get up, stagger to the shower, then load the kids and the other half of the unopened presents into the car, and drive to *your* parents' house, which is two hours *east* of yours. When your spouse says, "Are you too tired to drive?" you snap, "I'm not any more tired than you are."

9:00 A.M.: You unload the kids and the presents, and eat eggs, bacon, ham, sausage, Danish pastry, hash browns, coffee, and orange juice, which your mother has had ready since 7:00 A.M. ("We thought you might get here early.") She mentions every fifteen minutes that it's a shame that you couldn't have come yesterday and stayed overnight, but she supposes that (sigh) most of Christmas Day is better than nothing.

10:30 A.M.: You struggle valiantly to stay awake while everyone opens presents. Your father boasts that he's been up since 6:00 A.M. (as if you haven't) and says that in the old days you kids would be up at the crack of dawn to open your presents—none of this middle-of-the-morning stuff.

Noon: You spend all afternoon helping your mother fix an enormous Christmas dinner of turkey, ham, mashed potatoes, gravy, dressing, rolls, and mincemeat pie.

5:00 P.M.: You stuff yourself—again—while your mother says, "That's not all you're going to eat, is it?" Shelley Winters and Raymond Burr are beginning to look anorexic compared with you.

9:00 P.M.: You help your mother clean the kitchen. Then you load the kids and the now-opened remaining half of the presents into the car and drive two hours back to your house. The kids are asleep before the car leaves the driveway. Your spouse—who doesn't bother to ask if you're too tired to drive—watches you silently with a terrified look that says, "We'll never make it home alive."

11:00 P.M.: You unload the kids and the last half of the presents, and as the kids stumble up to bed, one of them says, "How come we never get to spend Christmas at our house?"

In your best holiday voice, you say, "Shut up."

What's Wrong with This Picture?

Holidays are supposed to be fun, but many of you aren't having a good time. If you spend the holidays at your own house, your parents aren't happy, because you're not with them. If you *do* spend your holidays with them, your parents aren't happy, because you don't stay long enough. If you split your time between your parents and your spouse's parents (one couple I know drives from Maryland to Tennessee, and then commutes 170 miles back and forth between their respective parents' houses in Nashville and Knoxville), your parents are downright insulted.

You run yourself and your family ragged trying to make your parents happy, and it doesn't work.

The Tug of War

Every year you battle it out with your parents, your spouse's parents, and your conscience about where you're going to spend the holidays. The decision is usually based on one or more of the following criteria:

1. Which parents scream the loudest if you don't spend the holiday with them. (Nice guys—and nice parents—finish last.)

2. Which parents have done the most for you in the past year. (Don't bother to keep track; they'll provide a tally for you.)

3. Which family has the most other people coming: "But, dear," your mother says, "the whole family will be there. You'll be the only one missing."

4. Which family asks first: "I'm sorry, Mom," you say, "we were going to come there, but Bob's mother called and asked if we'd made plans yet, and I didn't know what to tell her, because we hadn't talked to you yet, and..."

5. Which family is neediest: "I'm an only child," you tell your spouse. "We have to spend Christmas with *my* parents."

Our Family Is the Only Family

What causes all these problems is the True Family concept. In your parents' mind, *their* nuclear family (themselves, you, and your brothers and sisters) is the only family that counts. It is the True Family, the center of the universe around which all other relationships revolve.

Your spouse and children don't count—they're just a subset of the True Family. Even your parents' parents, what's left of them, are now just hangers-on who must go along with whatever the True Family (i.e., your parents) decides.

The fact that you have in-laws is, at best, an inconvenience. That they might also want to see you over the holidays is irrelevant. That your spouse might want to spend time with his or her parents is inconsiderate.

Your first loyalty is to the True Family that your parents have worked so hard over the years to put together.

No More Holidays on the Interstate

You've got to overcome this conditioning. Your first loyalty is to *your* family: yourself, your spouse, and your children. If you feel like going to the Bahamas and spending Christmas with neither set of parents, that's your right.

Your parents want you to believe that you have the power to totally and completely ruin their holidays, but it just ain't so.

Christmas may be the most important day of the year to your father (as your mother tells you weekly starting in July), but Father is a big boy now, and he will survive if you do Christmas the way *you* want to.

Holiday Planning—Adult-Style

What you do for the holidays will depend on whether you have children, where your parents live, where your spouse's parents live, and how well you get along with all these people. But here are a few guidelines:

Christmas is for kids. If you have children, stay put instead of roaming the countryside like a pack of gypsies.

Spend Christmas Eve from 6:00 P.M. until Christmas Day at noon in one place—preferably your own house.

If a big family Christmas at Grandma and Grandpa's farmhouse in Vermont is what everybody enjoys, go for it. But what's best for your children far outweighs what your parents want. Don't drag the kids all over the country just to make your parents happy.

Apply the Equal Time Rule. Spend Thanksgiving with one set of parents and Christmas or Hanukkah with the other. Then alternate this schedule every year. Be fair. Don't spend every Christmas with your parents because they bought you your house, or with your spouse's parents because they throw the biggest fit if you don't.

Celebrate the holidays en masse. For in-town parents, consider getting everybody (your parents, in-laws, kids, cousins, etc.) together at whoever's house is biggest. Then let everyone bring a portion of the meal, and give each person a specific assignment for clean-up.

Make a decision and stick to it. Whatever you decide, announce it to both sets of parents, and tell them it is fixed, permanent, and irrevocable. Revise it only in the event of extraordinary circumstances, such as a parent being widowed, or all twenty-three members of the family getting together for the first time in ten years.

14

It's All Up to You

GETTING ALONG with your parents is a challenge—no doubt about it. But once you get rid of all the old information, old attitudes, and old habits you've been dragging around with you for years, you'll find that it's not as difficult as it seems.

Because the bottom line is that your parents will behave only as well as you demand they behave, and they'll misbehave just as badly as you let them. If you insist that they conduct themselves like reasonable, civilized human beings, they probably will. If you let them get away with anything and everything, they'll do that, too. So:

- Don't act like a child around your parents. Turn down the handouts, the coddling, and all your parents' attempts to put you back in the cradle.

- Treat your parents with the same kindness, friendliness, and self-restraint that you use with your friends. And ask your parents to return the favor.

- Stand up for yourself. Don't tolerate insults, intimidation, or any other behavior that upsets you.

- Don't let your parents run your life, and don't try to run theirs.

- Stop thinking that your parents' happiness is your responsibility.

- Lighten up. Stop taking your problems with your parents so seriously, and you might find out that those problems aren't as big as they seem.

Hey, nobody said it was going to be easy. Your parents aren't in any big rush to change this relationship. They're in the habit of treating you like a child, and habits are hard to break. But if you act like a self-respecting adult (emphasis on the *adult,* and extra emphasis on the *self-respecting),* your parents, sooner or later, will learn how to treat you like one.

You know exactly the kind of relationship you'd like to have with your parents, and you should never stop working toward that goal. And if you're raising a family (or plan to), you should keep that ideal behavior in mind, because eventually *you* will be on the *parent* end of this scenario.

Someday You'll Have Adult Children, Too

It is inevitable: As we grow older, we turn into our parents.

You glance in a storefront window, and instead of seeing your own reflection, you see your father or your mother looking back at you. You talk to your children exactly the way your parents talked to you—even though you swore you'd never do it: "What kind of moron leaves a glass of milk under his bed for a week? Well? Are you going to answer me? *Are you?*"

And twenty years from now, you'll be saying to them, "What do you mean you're not coming out to visit this summer? We haven't seen you since Christmas. Can't you at least send the kids? No? Well, why don't we come there for two or three weeks? Wouldn't that be fun?"

Even though you swear you'll never do that, you will. You'll do all the things your parents do now.

To help keep that day as far off in the future as possible, here's a list of reminders. Stash it away somewhere, to be opened on your child's twenty-fifth birthday (twenty-one is too young; you won't be ready to let go yet), and read carefully by both you and your spouse.

(This list, by the way, is suitable for framing, should you decide to tear out these few pages and give them to *your* parents now.)

CREDO FOR THE PARENTS OF ADULT CHILDREN

Respect. I promise to treat my grown children with the same respect and courtesy that I treat my friends. I will try to stop thinking of them as "my babies," a free source of labor, or inferior human beings.

Advice. Before I give my children advice, I will ask myself if I've given it before. If I have, I will assume my children heard me the first time, and I will stop repeating myself.

Knowledge. I will remember that although I knew a lot more than my children when they were five, now that they're thirty, we're about even.

Honesty. I promise to deal honestly with my children. I will tell them the truth about how I feel and what I want. Somehow I will learn to take no for an answer.

Self-Pity. I will help my children remember my birthday, Mother's Day, Father's Day, our anniversary, and any other important events. I will not look for ways to feel sorry for myself or ways to make my children feel guilty.

Money. I will let my children know exactly what they can expect from me in the way of financial support for college, weddings, and loans.

About their inheritance, I will tell them, "With luck, the

day I die will be the day I spend my last cent"—so they can see me as a person and not as a potential windfall profit.

Visits. I promise not to say, "When are you coming to see me?" more than four times a year.

I will arrange all visits with my children by letting *them* decide when I should come and how long I should stay. And I will never stay longer than a week—no matter how far away they live.

I will remember that there is no such thing as a parent who visits too seldom or goes home too soon.

Retirement. I will arrange for my own entertainment and support during my twilight years. I won't expect my children to provide it.

Home. I will never move in with my children. I won't let my grown children move back in with me (at least not for more than a month—well, maybe six weeks).

My Children's Marriages. I will remember that my child's marriage is none of my business, and my son- or daughter-in-law is somebody's spouse, not my child.

And Finally… I will never, ever forget the problems I had with my parents, and when my grown children upset me, drive me crazy, or disappoint me, I will ask, "Is it me?"

About the Author

JANET DIGHT is a graduate of Ohio State University and a former marketing executive with Borden, Inc., and Kentucky Fried Chicken. She is now a full-time writer, living in Colorado Springs, Colorado. Her first book, *Breaking the Secretary Barrier,* was published in 1986.

Following the publication of *Do Your Parents Drive You Crazy?,* she will be busy trying to get back in her parents' good graces.

Her parents are busy compiling a list of ways she could do that.